Secrets on a Hill in Chocowinity, NC
Where a Predator Preyed
By Robin Ess

Prologue

The year was 2002. I was a student at Indiana Purdue University studying philosophy and anthropology. I was divorced with 4 children and in a relationship that was holding on by a thread. On my way to campus one day, I suddenly had tunnel vision. It was like I was looking through a peephole. When I walked across campus, it was as if I were in slow motion. I thought the walls were caving in all around me when I stepped on the elevator. I could not breathe. When I finally arrived at the class, my whole body trembled from the inside out. It was bad. I couldn't hold a pen steadily because my hands trembled uncontrollably... That's pretty much how I ended up in therapy the first time.

The funny thing about trying to get away from whatever you're running from is that the whole time you're running away, you're so busy looking back to make sure whatever you're running from hasn't caught up that you steadily run into new sets of misfortune. I have always been running.

I felt consistently tired, tried, angry, disappointed, unprotected, unloved, suicidal, out of control, generally disgusted, and at the end of my rope for most of my 20s through late 40s (I am 53 now). I wore black on purpose back then. I mourned everything. I mourned what should have been but never was.

The past resurfacing was the opening of a can of worms waiting for their chance to escape. Amid a severe bout of self-diagnosed depression, I was forced to look at memories I had buried on purpose long ago. I'd patted them down to suppress them. One thing ol folk say about pressure is it bursts pipes. One day, the pressure of everything I'd tried to forget exploded all around me and from that moment on, life was a daze. To eyes that didn't know better, I was well put together. Little did they know I was holding on by a thread that was dangling.

My friend LaToya encouraged me to seek professional help. She said I needed help with processing my thoughts and feelings. Up until that point, I had never even thought about therapy. I never saw therapy as embarrassing. I saw it as a weakness, but I made myself go.

I'm a proud woman, so the sign that said "Psych Support" real big on the door was a problem for me. I wondered who thought putting the words "PSYCH SUPPORT" in large font on the front door...real big was a good idea. In my world, no one wants to be seen going through that door. It made no sense at all. I sat in my car, willing myself to get out of the car and go through that door. Heavy tears hid behind my eyes as I opened the door. I walked through it, announced myself at the front desk, and was told to have a seat. I sat, willing myself to remember to breathe and not to cry. I looked around and noticed that something was off.

3

People in the waiting room were rocking, tapping their feet or fingers, and making loud outbursts. Naturally I told myself that those people were way more worse off than me. I got to thinking that maybe I was in the place Everything about this doctor's office was dusty I wondered if I looked dusty too.

I can't remember my first therapist's name. I believe it was Julie. She was a young white girl. Real laid back. She painted her nails during my appointment. I entered her office for the first time. I noticed that the office was bright and airy. She introduced herself and asked me to come in and have a seat. She got right to the point,

"So, why do you think you are here?"

She asked, looking casually at me.

"To fix me,"

I replied

"What do you think needs fixing?"

she asked.

"Me. I am broken from a lack of a mother's love."

I replied.

She straightened up in her chair and asked,

"Do you have symptoms?"

That's when I told her how sometimes I feel like I'm outside of myself watching and how I'd become detached and isolated, and about my experience when I arrived on campus that day. I watched to see her reaction.

She simply said, "Well, those are symptoms,"

I told my therapist my story and confided how I felt when I told Gail what happened to me when I was a little girl and her cold-hearted response had been,

"If he never did it to me, why should I think he did it to you?"

I didn't speak to Gail for over a decade behind that statement.

Gail was the one person I thought would always have my back. I was wrong.

I told my therapist how I tried to tell Dan what Jackal did only to have him say (twice),

"I don't wanna talk about that. I don't wanna talk about that."

I explained to the therapist how I can recount what was said and done like nobody's business…but I have never remembered the specifics of the molestation. I told the therapist how I had very few memories of being in elementary school. Most people I know can remember who their favorite elementary school teacher was. My first memory of my teachers' names is in middle school; even then, it's foggy. My therapist told me that in many cases, a person, especially a child, often blocks out memories they don't want to remember. I told my therapist how when my girlfriends and I got together and talked about our first sexual experiences, they all talked about how painful it was and how they bled. I sat quietly listening, not understanding why I didn't feel pain and didn't bleed. I took a deep breath. It was all too much. I sat, crying silent tears in front of a stranger. I cried from the most profound depth of my spirit. The deeper we delved into my story, the more she'd tell me,

"It's amazing how well adjusted you are, considering your unstable foundation.

Chapter One / The Great Escape

Somehow my mother tricked me into questioning my sanity. Had me halfway believing I made up a story accusing an innocent man of being a child molester.

Mama said it never happened. She said she never slapped me across my face and told me that Jackal was her man. She said I made it up because I was a spoiled child who couldn't get my way about something. I stood perplexed, trying to remember a time I was spoiled.

I struggle to string together memories from a childhood that are all but forgotten, but for bits and pieces. Hindsight is an interesting thing. My earliest childhood memory is when I was a little girl in Blounts Creek, North Carolina. I remember a black car that looked like the one Batman drove in the movie, speeding down the dirt road, kicking up all kinds of dust as it sped towards Grandmama's house. The driver had to be headed to either

Grandmama's or Uncle Ray's house because those were the only homes on the dirt road. Mama and Grandmama hurried my oldest sister Gail, my baby brother Daniel, and my baby sister Amiee into the pantry. We had to be very quiet. I heard a car door open and then closed. Then I heard someone walking around and around Grandmama's house. I didn't know who it was or what they wanted. All I knew was that mama was scared. Finally, I heard the driver get back in the car and drive away.

The next time I saw that car, it was parked outside Grandmama's house. I was in the living room looking out of the screen door. A man got out of that car, walked up Grandmama's steps, and came to the door. He didn't knock. I didn't run. I stood there. I was just a little girl.

The man said,

"Unlock the door Robin. Come on baby, unlock the door."

So, I did. I unlocked the door. The stranger rushed past me, ran through Grandmama's house, grabbed my baby brother Daniel, and then took off to his car. He ran right past me. As he sped down the road with my brother in tow, Grandaddy stood in the middle of the road shooting at that black car.

Sometime later, we were all downtown Washington, NC. Mama, Gail, Daniel, me, and Grandmama stood in front of this great big building with steps going up all around the front. I don't know what happened inside that building that day, but Daniel was back with us when we left to go back to Grandmama's house. I would later learn that my father was the man in the black car. He'd kidnapped Daniel and not me. The truth is, I had a father and a bunch of cousins less than 2 hours away. They were replaced with Jackal.

I can't remember when it began, the touching. I just know Jackal had me in his lap every chance he got. He liked to wrestle and play. Jackal liked pinning me. I remember the tan shorts he had on when I looked down and saw his penis. I remember catching him outside the bathroom window…watching. I remember him playing and falling on top of me. I remember him coming into our room at night, fondling, doing what a good man would never do. All this while pretending to be a good father."

It came to a head one day. I'm not sure how old I was when mama took me to Daniels's bedroom. To this day, the only thing I remember was mama slapping me across my face and saying, "That's my man!

Mama married Jackal when I was too young to remember. I have seen photos though. They got married at Grandmama's house in Blount's Creek. We were a perfect family to eyes that didn't know any better. We went everywhere together. We watched TV together. We played monopoly together and put on shows in the house together. Mama cooked breakfast, lunch, and dinner. We all sat at the table and ate together. It was our norm. When all you know is one way, it's easy to believe that what you know is normal. Describing my childhood as sheltered would be an understatement. I never had friends over. I never went anywhere with my friends. If it wasn't about school, it wasn't happening. I have never even gone to a sleepover.

When I was a senior in high school, the reins on me were loosened because of prom and graduation stuff. Other than that, we were in the house. Daniel was the only boy. He was allowed to ride a bike, go up the road, and hang out with his friends. I didn't know what a double standard was back then, but I knew there was one where Daniel was concerned.

In middle school, there was a kickball game between students and teachers. I watched from the bleachers. John, one of my classmates, was listening to a song on the radio I'd never heard. I asked him where he got it from. He said,

"The radio."

He looked at me like he thought I was playing. I wasn't. My life was in that little house on that little hill in Chocowinity, NC, on Gray Road, where we were not allowed to touch the radio. We listened to whatever Mama and Jackal played. We didn't have cable TV. Mama had us watching "Hee-Haw" and the "Lawrence Wilkes Show." We listened to old albums from back in the day while there was a whole world outside that we were not a part of. I watched other children do things I was never taught or allowed to do. I can barely ride a bike and can't skate at all. My classmates went to the skating rink all the time. They did stuff. They went places. I was home with Mama, Jackal, Gail, and Dan. It was just us. Rarely did anyone visit, and on the rare occasion when guests did visit, Gail, Daniel, and I naturally went to our rooms. We didn't come out unless summoned.

"Sing that song" or "dance that dance,"

Mama would say.

We naturally obliged. Mama always had a way about her. She was hateful and sweet at the same time. One minute Mama would use the broom handle and pretend it was a microphone. She would sing and dance and perform for us children. In the next minute, the cut of her eyes and the tone of her voice were completely different. She is eccentric, and I don't think she knows it. As a child in the early 80s, I recall my mother taking my sister Gail and me to a resale shop for school clothes shopping. It was like an old-timey flea market. Mama bought Gail and me outfits from the same era as the TV show "Little House on the Prairie..." bonnet and all. To my knowledge, "Little House on the Prairie" clothes have never been fashionable. At the time, it never seemed odd though. It was just what it was. I think a person who is always surrounded by people is afraid of being alone, and a person who doesn't have friends is hiding something or doesn't know how to be a friend...or both.

Mama was a loner. I never knew her to have a friend until she was in her 60s. I remember smiling at her and saying,

"Aww, Mama, you got a friend."

I vaguely remember mama taking Gail and me to the Dr. I remember my pee stinging. I remember the discomfort of the Dr. performing an examination.

When I was a senior in high school, Jackal and Mama took Gail and me to a building in downtown Washington, NC. I remember because it was raining. I had on my favorite yellow raincoat. It was the same day I got my glasses. Everyone went through the door before mama and me. Right before I went in, mama grabbed my arm and said,

"Robin, when you go in there, they will ask you to write your name on a piece of paper, and when they do, you write the word on this paper as your last name."

Mama handed me a little sheet of paper with the word "Caurel" written on it. I was confused because my last name was Moore before that day, and I had never heard the name "Caurel" before. So many questions ran through my mind, but you don't question mama. I went into the building and signed what I later discovered was an adoption form. Mama let Jackal adopt me, Gail, and Dan. Amiee was his biological daughter. I never did ask mama about that little piece of paper. Mama had no right to deny her children knowledge of their father and then pass a child predator off as a replacement.

I remember Jackal loving this singer name Denice Williams. She sang the prettiest song called "Silly" Jackal went out and bought her album. To this day, I still don't know how mama put a big hole in that album...but she did

Everything from those days is a blur, bits, and pieces turning over here and there. My high school graduation found me in a mental mess. I don't know how I felt, but I knew that my experience and my classmates' experience were two different experiences. My classmates were happy and carefree. I was just going through the motions waiting for it to be over. I'd had enough. I can't remember a single bit of my graduation. I couldn't tell you who sat to my left or right. I felt numb while my classmates were out celebrating, riding up and down the road, justa blowing their horns and having all kinds of fun. I lay on my bed, knowing it would only be a matter of time before I left for college. I was one step from freedom, and I knew it. I distinctly remember that moment.

Mama played the "proud Mama" when Gail and I went off to Winston Salem State University. Gail is a year older than me. We share the same birthday. I hated sharing my birthday with Gail when we were little. I didn't understand why I couldn't have my own cake. Gail sucked her thumb until it was flat and smelled like spit. One year I distinctly remember mama letting

Gail help her make our birthday cake. It must have been around Easter because the cake was shaped like a bunny rabbit. I watched Gail cut one of the round cakes into the bunny's ears. Then she had to pick it up and connect it to another round cake that was supposed to be the face. I'm pretty sure that's when my strong dislike for people touching my food kicked in. I don't understand why mama didn't just make cupcakes or separate the layers of the cake into two separate cakes. Why would I want my birthday cake to be prepared by someone who sucks their thumb? How is wanting your own birthday cake selfish…. when everybody else gets their own?

Gail graduated a year before I did. To this day, I don't know what Gail was doing during my senior year of high school. I know that when I went to college, she was right there. I remember thinking that if mama expected me to go off to college and live in a dorm room with my sister, who I shared a bedroom with at home… I'd just assume not to go to college at all. I was prepared to figure out a plan B. I remember getting irritated with mama right before she and Jackal left from dropping Gail and me off at WSSU. Mama pulled me aside and told me to look out for my sister like I was the oldest. I loved my sister, but my college experience should have been mine and mine alone like all my friends. That was my experience that she piggybacked on. If her heart was set on going off to college, why would she wait

13

a year and go where I went?

All I wanted was to leave home and go off alone as everyone else did. This is the first time I have expressed how that situation made me feel. Mama and Jackal bought Gail a microwave and a little refrigerator for her dorm room. I remember being so excited because I just knew their next stop would be dropping mine off at my room on the 4th floor. (Looking back on it, they had to pass the 4th floor to get to Gail's room on the 6th floor). It never happened. My refrigerator and microwave never showed up. When I asked mama why I didn't get a microwave and a refrigerator, mama said,

"Gail needs it more than you do Robin. You know how you are. You make friends easy."

I didn't protest. I did wonder what my personality had to do with the fact that one got some and one didn't. To this day, her logic at that moment baffles the shit out of me.

I watched Mama and Jackal leave after they dropped us off at WSSU. I didn't know what to do with myself. I was free. So naturally, I went buck wild. I did everything except for what I was supposed to be doing. I lost my virginity to an older firefighter. I was ditching class. He introduced me to his family and had me hanging out and being grown, and I loved every minute of it. My grades fell, and before I knew it, the semester was over, I was on academic probation, and it was time to go back home. As Gail and I waited for Mama and Jackal to pick us up to go back to Chocowinity, all I could think was, "Under no circumstances will I be trapped in that house again:

RUN LITTLE GIRL

Run, little girl,
as fast as you can
until you reach that distant land.
There will be people
who will understand,
run, little girl,
as fast as you can.
Fight, little girl,
with all your might.
Don't worry about what's wrong.
Fight for what's right.
Fight, little girl,
with all your might.
Have faith, little girl,
with all of your soul,
even when you are 100 years old...
when your belly is empty,
and

your hands are cold.

Have faith, little girl,

with all

your soul.

MAMA

Sometimes I sit and cry no apparent reason why no matter how hard I try, the same question lingers. "Why?" Time has passed. I feel the same, a child who never knew her name. Mother held back the love her little girl lacked. Father less than a man, doing things a child couldn't possibly understand. Creeping in at night, never chasing away the fright. A touch that was so cold from a man so old, leaving tales to unfold I will not be my mama's mold. Sweet home to an outsider was the center of the divider that tore my heart apart. When did it start? A yard so big with all those trees and woods brought me to my knees. Violated all in the name of love because this man fitted you like a hand fits a glove. What of me? See my eyes? Remember my smile? Inside…I didn't feel worthwhile. I left that place…put it out of my mind. The real me…I'm still trying to find. Writing, a gift I got from you, Writing…My love that's true. All the pain flows from my head. Days wishing I was dead. Tears left their stains on my face…from pain that even you can't erase. I miss the way

I wanted it to be, instead...reality. You were not there when I needed you the most. So, I traveled to a different coast, searching for anything to make me complete. Love was dull, null, void, and obsolete. I have dealt with more than any woman should endure. It all began with a home that was less than pure. Too many names, the sad shame. I have to lift this burden from my heart. Find a better place to start to forgive the person you taught me to be in an attempt to change reality. Sad songs touch my soul, fill me with remorse, and make me cold. Trust? I don't know it. The past? I have let go of it. All those times, I tried to do what I thought you thought was right, only to end up in a fight. You thought I was a tramp, some kind of a whore. What would you think that for? That man of yours had no right creeping in the middle of the night. What of you? What was in your head when you left my soul for dead? The smile on your face can't be real. You are my mother...you know how I feel.

FOR THE LOVE OF MY CHILDREN

For the love of my children,
I would lay down my life,
deprive myself of becoming a wife,
go without food, water, and rest...
to make sure that they are safe in the nest,

17

walk for miles up a mountain…

Swim for days in the cold,

then fall to my knees

and beg the Creator,

"PLEASE!

Show me the way that a MOTHER should be.

PLEASE walk this path with me

that has so many twists and turns

and so many new lessons

that have to be learned."

For the love of my children,

I will go down in the pit

to make sure that they are healthy and fit.

To make sure that they will not endure life's bullshit

that constantly threatens to overtake the day

to make muddy,

an otherwise clear way.

For the love of my children,

there is nothing that I would not do,

because the love between us

is the only thing true.

DISMAL DAY

My mother died today.

In my heart,

she melted away,

melting over time.

The pain is mine for life.

She never sacrificed for me,

only birthed me into this dismal existence

where resistance is futile,

and meanwhile,

I carry on because that is what I'm supposed to do,

not what I want to do.

I just want to lay it down

and

not be bound to this place anymore.

I gotta be careful what I wish for

cause I just might get it

and all the other shit I didn't consider.

DO YOU KNOW?

Do you know what today is?

Do you know what I know?

Let me tell you what today is.

Today is the day that I must go.

Why must I climb the mountain?

Why must I swim the sea?

A mountain as high

as the clear blue sky,

a sea that's as deep as it can be.

When I get over the mountain,

what, then shall I do?

I'll look to see how high I am,

and

then I'll reach my hands out to you.

EYES

Eyes are the key to the soul,

watching life unfold,

memorizing every mold from hot to cold.

Eyes see the future and the past

They grow old too fast.

Eyes reflect joy and pain,

 the wise,

the insane,

an invisible chain to the soul

as they watch life unfold.

Eyes reflect true emotion

in the tears they cry.

To see my soul,

look into my eyes.

BIRTH

Forming all by myself

with the assistance of the outsider,

who provides my everything.

Helpless within the womb,

being consumed

with the fluids that sustain my life,

growing and knowing that the unknown is near,

not knowing the meaning of fear,

suddenly I can move…

I can move!

The outsider knows I'm here.

Will it comfort me?

That's right…

I know no fear.

Not knowing the concept of time…

I can feel the time is near.

Preparations have been made.

My world is changing…

It's rearranging.

I'm slipping.

I try to hold on…

because suddenly…

I know fear.

No matter how hard I try,

I can feel my world crumbling…

from the inside.

I try to hide,

yet,

I can feel myself being pushed

rushed to somewhere.

Where am I going?

What will I see?

I can feel the souls drifting away from me…

no longer gripping me,

leaving me on my own,

being replaced with distorted souls…

looming on the outside

with the outsider…

in the midst.

The water is clear no more.

It's changed to the brightest red…

only I don't know red…

all I know is the water has changed.

It's not warm here.

It's cold,

and I am so alone.

Ooh...

to breathe this strange place

with all these strange faces

looking down on me,

yet, they cannot see...

What's to become of me?

I am born

THIS SMILE

This smile is not real. It does not represent the way I feel. This smile hides a look of despair. This smile goes on even when no one cares. This smile appears even when I want to cry. This smile is evident when my soul wants to die. This smile is polite and appears to shine, though it is not real...This smile is mine.

DESPAIR

Crying eyes filled with tears...

express fear.

Unsteady hands...

no one understands

life's harsh demands.

Deep in thought…

a hurting heart

when the crying starts…

hearts torn apart.

Eyes shut tight

to hold back the fight,

rumbles within

to handle the sin,

problems with the soul

since days of old.

A heart is cold,

as the mystery unfolds.

It began with

a mother and father

that never took time to bother

with a child who was not to blame

who never even knew her name.

MEEK

Why must we suffer so deep within

for our faults and sins?

If we ask for forgiveness,

why can we not forget?

Why must we feel

such a great sense of regret?

If another soul hurts our heart,

how can we not care

if we know that the pain we feel

is the pain another put there?

If trust is broken,

are we expected to overlook the loss

of a closeness that was once between us

that was taken away at no cost?

If another soul takes from us,

why are we expected to turn the other cheek

and remain forgiving and meek?

Chapter Two / When the Bough Breaks

After doing everything except for what I was supposed to be

doing in college and after being put on academic probation, all I

could think was,

"I gotta get up out of my Mama's house."

The goal was to get as far away as possible. So, when a friend

asked me to ride with her to Raleigh, NC, where she would take the ASVAB test to join the Air Force, I was all for it until we got there, and I realized I didn't have anything to do while she took her test. My solution was to take the test too. So, I joined the United States Navy.

The memory that stands out to me is waking up on Halloween morning, knowing I was leaving to go to boot camp. I don't know what I expected...maybe some type of fair well. I found myself alone. I thought they were all hiding and waiting to jump out and wish me a fine farewell. I looked in the closets. It soon set in that there would be no farewell. No one stayed to see me off. I shook off my feelings of disappointment, and off I went to Orlando, Florida, for Boot Camp...this was like in 1989.

Joining the military was a complete and total accident. It should never have happened. I had no business in or with the US military. It is one of those things that, when you look back on it, all you can do is shake your head. I'm the last person who should have ever enlisted in the Navy. First, I can't swim, and most of all. I'm not going to be bossed about.

I joined the Navy with the sole intention of traveling to Japan and living there. I have no idea where that notion came from, and it didn't matter because Uncle Sam had a different plan in store for me. He sent me all the way to South Carolina. There I was, trying to escape North Carolina, and these fools sent me one state over. I wanted to be an engineer so that I could get a job making good money when I got out of the Navy. But oh no, Uncle Sam said that I would be a Storekeeper. A Storekeeper! So naturally…I rebelled. It bothered me that the recruiter lied to me and said I'd get to pick three places to be stationed. He had the nerve to call it my wish list and guaranteed I would get stationed at one of them. At no time did I select Charleston, South Carolina. As far as I was concerned, all bets were off. I had an attitude too strong to be contagious.

Before I arrived in Charleston, SC, I knew that the United States Navy would not get a day of good work out of me. They didn't, and it backfired. Before I knew it, I was undesignated. That means you're unemployed. Do you know what they call people in the Navy who have no job? A deck ape. So, I was in the Navy, beyond irritated, and being called a Deck Ape. I'm mad fire, and I knew it would be a long four years. The ship kept going underway. There were times when there was no land to be seen. Imagine the panic of constantly thinking the ship was sinking and knowing you couldn't swim.

One day the Senior Chief woke up on a whole different kind of stupid and thought it was a good idea to paint the outside of the ship (USS Sierra AD-18) during a storm in the middle of the ocean. What's worse is that he thought it was a good idea for someone to wear this little harness-type thingy while dangling over the side of the ship. The Senior Chiefs' bright idea was to throw one of us overboard, tied to what amounts to a thick rope. The instructions were,

" Take a paint bucket, brush, and paint outside the ship."

Never mind the fact that we were in the middle of the ocean during a storm. Nothing about his idea made sense. If I knew nothing else, I knew for a fact that it wouldn't be me. I knew he would say,

"Mills!"

and sho nuff he did.

I just stood there and looked at him for a few seconds and then asked,

"So, you *really* think I'm going to do that?

As I peered up at him, it became clear that he was dead serious. Before I knew it, I said,

"You must have lost your mind."

It was a legitimate question and statement to me, but to him, it was insubordination. I got in all kinds of trouble by asking a valid question and making a valid point. I went to a real-life court-martial and everything. Nothing became of it. It felt like a whole lot of play-play. I can't even remember who said what. The Navy's idea of punishment was to make me work in the kitchen. (They called it the galley). I didn't care. I wasn't going to be a deck ape, and I damn sure wasn't going to cook. I should have never taken that test to join the Navy. I just was killing time. In the end, it was my Great Escape from Chocowinity. What I learned about the Navy is that recruiters are liars.

One day, while bringing a fruit tray from the galley to the mess hall, I noticed this big buff chocolate Mandingo-type brother approaching me. As he got closer, I remember thinking that he looked better from a distance. He had frog eyes up close. I don't know what he said or how we ended up going out, but I do remember liking the notion of having my very own bodyguard. I was good for telling people,

"Don't make me go get Carter."

Carter was my daydream. I painted that man as a king in my imagination. We spent all our time together. I knew he was mean as a snake. Signs were shown early. I was just being stupid. I wanted to see what I wanted to see. There were plenty of chances to walk away, but I didn't. I got pregnant, and we got married. As the rules would have it, we couldn't be married on the same ship, so I opted out of the military early. Carter remained to finish up his last year. Everything happened so fast. Before I knew it, I was on the west coast, miles away from everyone I knew, living with my in-laws, who I had literally just met. In the beginning, everything was fine. I enjoyed Carter's Mother. We did everything together. Mrs. Carter and I used to paint by numbers before I even knew I could paint. I remember this one time Mrs. Carter and I were going somewhere (she was

29

driving), and then all of a sudden, she stopped driving like she was at a stop sign, only she wasn't...and while looking the other way, she asks,

"Do you see anything coming from that way? Mind you, the car was straddling a railroad track. I was like,

"Well, Mrs. Carter, would it matter if there was? Lol.

I got so tickled with her that day. Now I wonder if she thought she was scaring me. My ass was in the passenger seat, justa laughing.

Things didn't get bad until Carter left the Navy and came home as a civilian. Up until that point, his mother had been a complete doll. Little did I know she'd turn on me like a snake. The thing about military life is that people are different when they get out and get around their families. Carter arrived one day after the birth of our daughter Alley on September 21, 1990, and I was thrilled until I found out that Carter was a straight-up mama's boy. He had his mother telling me how to cook, clean, and raise our daughter. Mrs. Carter was getting on my last nerve. I wasn't having it. I remember telling Carter that he needed to choose a side because I was not about to be bossed about by his mother. This chick was relentless, and God rest her soul wherever it is, I will never forgive her. As a woman, I will never forgive Mrs. Carter. Her son did not need help being a hateful, hurtful, mean-spirited man. When Mrs. Carter realized I was the private type who didn't need to see her, her husband, or any of them except on occasion, she changed. She stopped being sweet, Mrs. Carter, and turned into the enemy. It's like when she realized I would raise my daughter how I saw fit without regard for her opinions...her sweet representative left the room. As far as I was concerned, Carter and I fucked raw and had that baby, and Mrs. Carter had nothing to do with it, so she should take several seats. When Mrs. Carter realized she could not run my house and that I was not backing down. I knew there would be a problem.

The last straw for me was when I was potty training Ally. I refused to give her some juice before dinner at one of Carter's family functions in Richmond, California. Mrs. Carter took it upon herself to overstep me as Alley's mother and give Ally juice, knowing I had already told her no. It was then that the concept of daycare came to my mind. Sending Ally to daycare would mean that Mrs. Carter would not be babysitting Ally anymore. My thought process was to eliminate any confusion. I would not allow my daughter to believe that Nana could override Mama. Mrs. Carter wasn't woman enough to back down. Things were never the same. I don't have one regret.

Almost a year and a half later, everything came to a head when I was nine months pregnant and two weeks overdue with our son. I was still working. Carter was laid off and had a hard time dealing with it. Between not having a job and comparing himself to his father, he took to drinking and became meaner and meaner. I tried to explain to Carter that it was an unrealistic expectation to compare himself to his father. I told him that Mr. Carter had his whole life to build his business. Carter would not listen to reason. It's like he was born miserable. I remember listening to him go on and on about being teased in school because his skin was dark. He complained about how crazy he looked when his mother gave him a Gerry Curl. He had the nerve to tell me that I was the darkest woman he would ever have because he did not want a dark-shined child. I don't know how I ended up wanting to be married to a man who truly hates being black. The beginning of our demise happened one day after I had gotten off from work. I was nine months pregnant and two weeks overdue. I was still working as CNA in a hospice home in Napa, California. It was a good little ride from Vallejo. There were days when I arrived home and didn't remember driving. I was exhausted. One day when I came home from work, all of Carter's "boys" were in our apartment playing whatever video game was popular in the '90s. I went to my typewriter to journal. I've always kept a journal. After I got done writing, I went to the bathroom to bathe. The evening is still a blur to me. I remember being in the bathtub and hearing Carter's brother ask him to drive him somewhere, and I called out, "Carter, take your car because you know I can't drive a stick."

My car was an automatic, and I knew I could drive it to the hospital if need be. The hospital was right around the corner. Carter was drunk and must have thought I was disrespectful. I was butt-ass naked in the bathtub when he burst in. Carter grabbed me around my throat, pulled me to my feet. I was dangling on my tiptoes, trying to breathe as he punched me in the face. Blood was everywhere. For the record, people do see stars when they get punched. Carter's brother, OlOdette, came running in. He had to pry Carter's hands from around my throat. All I remember before blacking out is Carter and his friends running down the steps, leaving my pregnant naked body on the floor bleeding. By the time I regained consciousness, I was in my neighbor's apartment in a robe meant to be worn by a little woman with short arms. Police cars and motorcycles were everywhere. My neighbor must have called the police when she found me naked on the floor with blood spilling from my face. I don't know how I ended up in her apartment. I remember hearing the police officers saying,

"You don't want to press charges against him. He's the father of your children."

Not one police officer tried to arrest that man who clearly put his hands on me.

I went back home with Carter. We went to bed. We went to sleep. When we awoke the next day, Carter went into the bathroom to shower. After showering, he came into our bedroom, acting as if nothing had happened, and casually asked, "Why didn't you clean up the blood?"

I was hurt figuratively and literally. I awoke to a swollen and bruised face. I felt myself become dangerous. Carter ripped that little line inside my mouth from my top lip to my gum and had the nerve to stand there as though nothing had happened, asking me to clean up the blood he spilled from my face. I saw red. I did the most loving thing I could have ever done for Carter. I picked up the phone and called His Mama and asked,

"Do you love your son?

She replied,

"Yes, of course, I love him."

Then I asked,

"Do you love him breathing?"

Before she answered, I continued,

"Can he come home?"

Carter and I never lived together again. I drove to Fairfield, California, picked up the divorce papers, got a lawyer pro bono, and filed for divorce. It broke my heart. A week later, I went into labor. Carter was a reservist. He claimed he was on duty in Hawaii. Mr. and Mrs. Carter were vacationing in Texas with family. I needed someone to babysit Ally while I had the baby, but I didn't know anyone. I was all alone with Ally, and all I

34

knew was that I had to get to the hospital. I did the only thing I could think to do at the time.

Through tears, I knocked on the neighbor's door who lived across the street with a bunch of kids and told her that I was in labor, wasn't from California, and didn't have anyone else to call. I explained that I needed someone to watch my child. She didn't even hesitate. She ushered Ally into her home and asked if I needed her to drive. I declined and drove myself around the corner to the hospital. What stands out most to me about the birth of my firstborn son was that while I was pushing him out into this world, the nurses kept asking me where my husband was. I told them that he was on duty. That's when one of the nurses informed me that Carter had picked up whatever paperwork he needed to be excused from duty for the birth of his son.

I was in labor. I was so angry. Our son Pauly was born beautiful and healthy to a mother who, unbeknownst to her, was in the throes of a deep depressive episode. It was as if everything around me was in slow motion. Not long after, Carter returned from wherever he was and had a sad sob story about how he had seen God on the beach and that God told him to go home and take care of his family. A part of me wanted to believe that he was serious. His actions showed otherwise. Mrs. Carter surprisingly came to see me. It was clear that the only thing that she was concerned about was my possibly moving back to NC with her granddaughter. She pulled out all the stops and ended with,

"Every marriage has those kinds of bumps in the road. You just have to wait it out."

I don't like to be told what I "have" to do. I recall being stunned that Mrs. Carter implied that Mr. Carter abused her back in the day. Then it made sense. When I first moved in with the Carters, Mrs. Carter and my sister-in-law Ro warned me that Mr. Carter was especially moody when he got off work. I watched Mrs. Carter and Ro scatter when Mr. Carter came through the door every day. So, this one time, I was downstairs when Mr. Carter came in. He went to the refrigerator and got a daily beer as usual. I stood at the island in the kitchen, munching on something. I sat down on the couch and thought to myself,

"He doesn't seem moody. He looks like he's having a beer in peace."

Mrs. Carter used her marriage as a shining example. She felt like she won because she waited him out. I told her that she and I were unalike because the first chance I got...I would get even. There would be no "wait." Mrs. Carter dropped the subject.

So, there I was, living in an apartment I could not afford with a one-and-a-half-year-old baby girl and a newborn baby boy. I somehow convinced the landlord to let me out of the lease.

Instead of charging me for breaking the lease, he charged Carter. My babies and I moved into an old studio apartment (it had a bed made in the wall) on Ohio Street in Vallejo, California. It turns out it had mice. Even though I was afraid of cats, my logic was that if I got a cat, it would kill the mice. So, I got a white cat named Mandy, knowing I was terrified of cats at the time. My logic worked, Mandy loved bringing me dead mice, and I almost had a heart attack every time.

One day the bank called me and alerted me that Carter was at the bank with a woman who pretended to be me, trying to cash our income tax check. The fool in me let it go I knew then that I was treading on dangerously thin ice and a step from snapping like a twig. So, what did I do? I invited Carter over and ran him a hot bubble bath like he liked and watched him submerge his body in the water and bubbles. Then I got the boom box and his favorite "Too Short" tape. I plugged the boom box up and intended to fry his ass. It was as if he read my mind because he got up from the water and wrapped the towel around himself while looking at me the whole time. I sat fearlessly, knowing that if I caught a case behind him, I could live with it. Carter should send me a card every year.... because if it wasn't for me, he would not be breathing.

Slowly but surely, I began to get back on my feet. I got a job as the assistant manager of a store called "Tandy Leather

Company" in Concord, California. Financially, I was barely making ends meet. I ended up getting food stamps. My mistake was thinking I could wait to report my income to the food stamp administration. Before I got a chance to report my new income, Carter took it upon himself to do it for me.

By then, I had relocated to Indianapolis, Indiana, on a job promotion with Tandy Leather. During that time, I received a letter from Marion County Social Services. The letter informed me that there was an overpayment and that I must report to court on a specific date to answer for myself. I was floored. It was my own fault for thinking I could get away with it. I know there is no "but," but even with a job, I was struggling. Carter was an abusive, non-supporting, attempting to starve, alcoholic, sorry excuse of a man who refused to buy food, diapers, pay for childcare, or anything for his children.

I was beyond irritated with Carter. Especially since he attempted to commit fraud by having a woman pose as me at our bank so he could keep our income tax money, and my dumb ass let him get away with it. I waived alimony. I knew enough that if I dealt with Carter's money, I would have to deal with him. Now to find out that he reported me to social services...and I had to fly all the way back to California and go before a judge with my children who had motion sickness on the plane. I don't know who I was more upset with, Carter for breathing or me for not h

business correctly. I did what I had to do.

I went before the judge and had a full-on panic attack

convicted of welfare fraud. I was shaking like a leaf from head to

toe. The attorney was concerned. I was just trying to breathe. I

didn't have to go to jail. I had to do community service. It was

my own fault. I had it coming, and I learned a valuable lesson:

You can't cut corners and expect to not deal with

consequences…and the good you do for others can come back

and slap you in your face. From then on, I saw Carter for

precisely who he was. A man who would do anything to get out

of supporting his children. Sure, he moved on with his life,

remarried, and had a child. Maybe he's not violent anymore. He

may be the perfect husband and father for all I know, but that

does not negate the monster he was in my life and the monster he

is in my dreams. Karma can be a slow bitch. Almost everything

and everyone he held dearly is gone. Until the day he dies, he

will eat, sleep, drink, and dream the karma he earned from

attempting to break my spirit.

GROWTH

Tides swell,

waiting to excel,

waiting to overflow to the shore.

Salty water stings the eyes,

burning them to their cores…

Hinders the process of growth.

SMOKE

I smoke cigarettes,

though I rarely have a lighter.

I sit and think and think…

Think about nothing…

or what it amounts to.

I go over it in my mind,

over in my mind

until I beat a path to my heart.

I hold back the tears,

hold back the tears,

hold the tears

until they weigh my heart down.

And yes,

I put it out of my mind,

put it out my mind,

I put my mind out…

Until I could not find it.

I ran from it,

ran from it…

ran…

Until it was right back in my face.

I looked the other way,

looked the other way…

looked away…

Cause I'm scared to face the fact…

That he loves another

JUST TO BE ABLE TO SAY "HUSBAND"

The man I married,

was some man I created in my mind.

The man I divorced

is some brotha I never even knew.

To flip the script so drastically is a trip,

got me tilting my head to the side…

Squinting and shit just to get a glimpse of him.

Then realizing that this was him all along…

I just would or could not see.

Ladies… If you're reading this,

Wake up.

JABBING AT WOUNDS

Did he ever really love me,
or was it all just a game?
Did he ever feel
how deep my love for him went?
Did he know how my heart leaped
or how it wept for him?
Does he know that the wound still hurts?
He can't know these things…
otherwise,
he wouldn't keep jabbing at the wounds.
Sometimes I want to scream
and kick
and then fall out
 and throw a temper tantrum
just for the hell of it.
Sometimes I cry and cry
until my eyes dry out…
just because and then sometimes,
my heart hurts and hurts…
because of the jab wounds in it.
I could see him dead
if I knew that it would not affect me.

He's still around…I see.

So, he'll die an old man

with a knife in his hand.

Jabbing at wounds,

he will never understand.

I never began to imagine that he never really loved me.

AKINDELE'

18 years ago

lost in time,

I still find myself reflecting over what is left

of the lies you tell

about stories I remember

all too well

about our demise

as I cried

and tried to hold false love together….

18 years have passed,

and the pain still lasts

from your hand to my face….

you, my drug laced with abuse,

and today it suits you to spin a tale

that I remember all too well…

18 years ago,

you closed your hand

and made a fist

could not resist drawing my blood

that led to floods of tears....

caused my worst fear came true....

cause there was a demon inside of you...

18 years ago,

you asked why I didn't clean up the blood that you spilled

that stemmed from a wound

that never did quite heal

because I believed you

when you preached about our forever.

I never dreamed

that you would ever tear away the seams

holding my love intact

and the fact that you act like it's all in my mind

causes me to find the time to put the truth in the air....

and I dare you to call my bluff....

cause I bout had enough

of your holier than thou disposition....

in your new position...

pretending to be a better man.

You better understand

I kept the police report

that reports the sort of man you secretly are…

and that I am by far stronger now…

can show you how better than I can tell…

can left my finger and cast a spell

and bring hell to your door…..

It's for sure….

Let one more word come back to me

about how I am blinded by anger

and refuse to see the past the way it was…..

and I'll bring more than pain….mutha fucker…

I'll bring the flood…

I divorced you.

While you sat in the back of the courtroom crying

and trying to get out of paying child support.

You need to abort this notion that you are better than me….

your punk-ass can't rewrite a history that was recorded

and a marriage that I aborted…

Told me that I was the blackest woman you would ever have….

said you didn't want a dark-skinned child.

Here it is 18 years later and what you got….

a nappy-headed mix child.

Say something! …

you abandoned your chance to apologize

when you filled the air with lies

and tried to paint yourself in a better light....

Read the police report Nigga....

that might clear your head

about the night you left me and our unborn Son

for dead...

when I was 9 months pregnant

and two weeks overdue...

broken hearted because of you....

Say something...I dare you.

And if anyone else wants to chime in

and cosign on your behalf....

let me say it now...real clear like...

Bitch, kiss my ass...

we talking bout a time before you....

I have no need to speaks words that are not true...

I don't know how they handle beef

on the other side of black...

but you better act like you know...

before I go to the airport

and get a ticket to come your way....

to look you in your face

to see you say some shit

that will have your ass missing

and me resisting arrest....

I guess I really am shitty…

such a pity…

y'all live on the west coast

in the city that is the bane of my existence….

where my resistance to the Carter was futile

and meanwhile….

I carried on….

went through storm after storm after storm

that only served to harm my heart.

Accident my ass…

say what you want, but you know my words are true

when I say…"NO good will ever stay with you"…

I could see you dead if I knew that it would not affect me.

You're still around…I see.

So, you'll die an old man

with a knife in your hand

jabbing at wounds

that you could never understand.,,

How dare you pretend that it was all a misunderstanding….

me laying on the floor in blood,

butt ass naked, and you standing there

with your brother

holding you back…

You better retract the lies you told.

Your debt is insurmountable,

and you will be held accountable

for the numerous times you tried to break my soul….

something that was never yours to control….

accident my ass…

no matter how much time passes…

the police report clashes with your recollection….

I'm sitting here today correcting you…

I commend you for changing your ways,

but it does not take back your misdeeds of yesterday.

You will still pay…

You continue to say,

"Stop bringing up the past"

I guess it's easy for you to say that stupid sounding shit

considering you were beating my ass…

Woooooaaaaah!

SHIPS

Ships that sail on the same sea

in the same fleet

shall never meet.

Waves carry each in the opposite direction

with no thought of correction.

The wind sings to each…
a different song.
Days and nights
linger much too long.
The sails explode with air,
chanting softly,
"I'll get you there."
Water swells with anticipation,
and I, the sailor,
am filled with frustration and suddenly,
left out on a limb
because I can't swim.

I HATE HIM

I hate him for being happy
while I lay stagnant.
I hate him for making plans for their future
while I contend with the day.
I hate him for being together
while I lay unraveling by the moment.
I hate him for being in love with her
though he promised himself to me.
I hate him for not caring

when he knew my world was in him.
I hate him for the tears I cry,
for broken ties,
and for not trying to keep us together.
I hate him for the back he turned
as my love burned out of control for him.
I hate him for forcing me to put him out
with my heart.
I hate him for the misuse and abuse
of my mind, body, and soul.
I hate him for living high on the hog,
for treating me like an old dog,
for drawing blood,
for causing harm,
and for perpetrating charm.
I hate him for causing me to grieve
after I was forced to make him leave.
I hate him for breaking my heart
when I really knew that it was goodbye
and for all the years I cried.
I hate him for leaving me alone
in a land that was not my home
but was his.
I hate him for forgetting about his seeds

and their needs until an unthinkable deed

forced him to see and be a man.

I hate him for doing so well without me.

I hate him for allowing me to love him completely

and never returning my love.

I hate him for breaking my heart and keeping it.

Chapter Three / Bad Rebound

So, there I was, a world away from where it all began. I was divorced and raising Ally and Pauly, all alone, sad, lonely, and needy—an easy target for a man looking for shelter and someone he could control.

He slipped in like a weed through a crack. Van came across as the perfect man who adored my children and me. Never mind that he was paranoid, addicted to weed, had more dreams than drive, and had a son in Kentucky he never saw or supported. Never mind the fact that with him, I was going through the motions just to be able to say, "my man." We played the "couple" role and were together for almost seven years.

I ended up relocating from California to Indianapolis, Indiana, for a job promotion with Alley, Pauly, and Van. By then, Van and I had two sons together, Malcolm and Darius. Van started out so kind and nurturing. Now he was controlling and argumentative. I should have seen the signs, especially when I noticed that Van had cut two holes in the curtains to peep out the window. If that was not enough, he was a mama's boy with a mother who undoubtedly was born from the pits of hell. I couldn't stand her. Overbearing was an understatement, and she was naturally argumentative. I overlooked all that and chose to make Van a king in my imagination.

Something about him didn't sit right with my spirit. The newness was gone. His representative had long since left the building. What was left was a simple-minded little man who overcompensated for shortcomings. I ignored his obvious character flaws. I pegged him to be many things, but I never pegged him to be a child molester. Van is my most profound regret.

It was 1998. One morning I quietly woke Ally, who was eight years old at the time, to see if she wanted to run errands with me. She excitedly got herself dressed and ready to go. We were sitting in Burger King when she said it,

"Mitchell and I have a secret."

As soon as she said it, I felt my heart stop. That's when she told me that Mitchell "touched" her. I can't even describe the feeling that washed over me. Everything went blank. I watched Ally's lips move as she changed the subject and talked about whatever little 8-year- old girls talk about. Ally didn't know it, but at that moment, something inside her mother snapped. Repressed memories of being molested by Jackal as a child came rising to the surface and crashing all around me. I could hardly breathe. I kept it together, though. I knew I had to act normal because the last thing I wanted was for Ally to think she'd done something wrong. The one thing I knew at that moment was that I would not be my mother's mold. I would believe my child. I played my anger off and acted normal. Ally and I went about our day. It took everything in me to keep myself together, knowing I would kill that son of a bitch when I got home.

Van was in the living room when we got back. I asked Ally to get Pauly from upstairs. The plan was to take them to my neighbor Kim's house to play with their friend, Brionna. Ally hurried upstairs and came back quickly with her brother. I yelled over my shoulder to Mitchell and told him I would be right back after I dropped the kids off at Kim's house to play with Brionna. He was none the wiser. I felt numb as I walked down the walkway to Kim's apartment. I don't remember knocking on the door. I remember Kim eyeing me up and down like she knew something was wrong. I told her what Ally had told me. It's like Kim read my mind and knew what I would do. She insisted that I calm down and told me not to do anything crazy. She sent her boyfriend Tim to my apartment instead. Tim lied to Van and told him there was a warrant for his arrest, and he had until Monday to turn himself in. It worked. Van turned himself in to the police the following Monday. That's how he ended up in prison.

The police sent Detective Gullion to investigate. The first thing he told me to do was take Ally to the hospital for an examination. The lab's finding was that there was no evidence of penetration or molestation. The investigation found no evidence to prove what Ally said Van did. I was devastated. There was no way this man would get away with what he did to my child.

Days later, Van wrote me a letter from jail begging me to let him come home and swearing he was sorry. He said that he touched Ally because he was molested as a child. He said he wanted to come home and get the help he needed to make it right. As I read the letter, I was livid. I never told Carter about the molestation in my whole marriage, but I told Van. Then he turned right around and did the same thing to my daughter, and there he was, begging to come home like it was a real possibility. All I knew was that the police had better keep him because he would wish they had if they let him go. Prison was the safest place for him. I gave the letter to the prosecutor, and Van was sentenced to 13 years. He left behind our two sons, Malcolm and Darius, who never knew their father as children. Van shattered what little faith and trust I had left in people to dust.

It's true what people say, "Blood is thicker than mud." Van's mother came to see me after he turned himself in. She pleaded with me to drop the charges. She said her son was sick and needed help, not jail. I was numb as I listened to her overlook that her son was a child molester who molested my child. She expected me to show grace and mercy by dropping the charges. I told her point-blank that Mitchell was where he was supposed to be and that she should be grateful. The next thing I knew, she was coming at me with her cane like she thought she was going to hit me with it. Never had I been so calm. I did not move a muscle when I said,

"I will beat your old decrepit ass if you take one more step towards me."

I meant every single word, and she knew it. She stopped in her tracks and threw on an outraged face, then flung herself around, ran from my apartment, and told all my neighbors that I threatened to kill her. I was so angry.

Dealing with what happened to Ally rehashed my past. It was too much for me. I was so angry with myself for not seeing the signs. It was more than I could take. I tried to be strong. I was flailing like a fish out of water, trying to hold on to anything to feel stable because I could feel myself slipping. There were times when the world was happening around me, and I was oblivious. It was like I checked out.

I was a full-time student at Indiana Purdue University studying Philosophy and Anthropology. I knew the bottom had fallen out and that I was skating on melting ice the last day I was on campus. I had tunnel vision. It was like I was looking through a peephole. The world stood still, and I was floating. The elevator ride to class lasted forever. It's like I was holding my breath without trying. By the time I finally got to class, I knew. I sat through my anthropology class to tell Dr. Mullen I wouldn't be back to class any time soon. I told him I wouldn't be able to participate in the archaeology dig because I had issues that needed tending.

That storm brewed for years. It can be said that depression is a monster that haunts conscious and self-conscious thoughts. I had been through pain that numbed me to the sensation of being. It was during that period that I became a recluse. I trusted no one and felt alone. After running the whole of my life, I was finally standing still, facing demons in the mirror. I'd spent my entire life needing someone or something, and for the first time, I was in a position where I was alone on purpose. I had a roommate when I was at WSSU. I lived with hundreds of people in the Navy, then I got married, then I had children, and then I was in a relationship. For me to have felt so alone, I didn't know what it felt like to live alone. A part of me was afraid of being on my own. But then, I wasn't on my own. I had four children by then. So, there I was, trying to make it on my own, processing thoughts and contending with the day with the world's weight on my shoulders. I started having severe panic attacks. Though I wasn't a good candidate for therapy, therapy was my support. I like to mess with people sometimes. My favorite answer to the question the therapists asked was,

"Well, who hasn't?"

I was asked questions like.

"Have you ever been depressed for more than three days at a time? Have you ever felt isolated? Have you ever had homicidal thoughts? Have you ever had suicidal thoughts? Do you have periods when you cannot sleep?"

The questions went on for what seemed to be forever. Based on my answers, I was a certified nutcase from the sound of things.

I remember feeling as defeated as anyone could be. I was broken. My grasp of reality was not firm. I wasn't fully present. I was dangling. Days and nights lingered and mixed, I never knew what day it was, and sleep was not an option. I painted a whole townhouse ...upstairs and downstairs, in three different colors in one week. I am the queen of nesting. I've changed the furniture around every other week. I was manic before I knew what manic was. I had no appetite. I was going through the motions of breathing.

My biggest regret is that I broke down, and my children had to live through it with me. I was detached. I was in mourning for something I never knew. I hid in the bathroom. I always bounced back, but I always revisited my sad place. To this day, my children tell me the best stories I was a part of, and no part of me remembers. I was clearly functioning at times. If I could change one thing. I would have been a better mother.

I knew I needed to pull myself together. I cried for what seemed like forever in therapy. My cheeks stung from the salt of my tears. My therapist looked genuinely concerned. I have always kept a journal. I let my therapist read my journal to better understand my mind's workings. A month later, in a different, more confident state of mind. I sat in the same chair in the same office, talking to the same therapist. This time I had a better grasp of reality and could clearly convey my feelings. I expressed my overall lack of enthusiasm for the concept of living. I explained that, in my case, life seemed like one cruel joke after another. I explained that I felt trapped living until I died, and even then, no one really knew what was next. I explained that there is a difference between negative thoughts and an accurate assessment of one's reality. She did not refute my opinions. She gave me words of encouragement and told me that life would not look so bleak if I continued to do the work. She gave me some cute little pills she said would calm my nerves and give me a better perspective when negative thoughts entered my mind. I was popping Neurontin, Seroquel, and Depakote, and those are just the ones I remember.

THE THERAPIST SAID

It's been a minute since I last sat down to get down.

The flare went out…

Now, reappears…

through laughter through tears.

No fears to report.

I'm not caught up or out of sorts.

Stress…remains….at a minimum in the new millennium.

The Therapist says there is a cure for my disorder.

Gonna make me "pure,"

says I should study meditation and marination..

Said I have too much on my plate

that I complicate my own fate

with shit it can't possibly eat…

Fighting defeat.

Said I seem so bright…

like a shining light…

that I could be a doctor,

or some shit that she thinks is "great."

If only I would take charge of my fate.

Said she has the hookup…

can't wait to put me on my path.

Said she had the calm for my aftermath.

Yes, that Dr. said a whole lot of shit that I couldn't let you miss.

Saying shit like…

"Does it feel like your mind is going faster than your mouth?"

Causing me to stop…reflect…then smile…

cause I checked…It's true!

My, my, my, what can I do?

Close my mouth, pick up my pen, and think of some shit for my

mind to get in.

EXCAVATION

The excavation unearthed a vision that is real,

caused me to feel trepidation

about this new exploration

I embark, like a flashlight in the dark…

making my mark to show the way.

Today the most fulfilling

and frightening sensation

pauses my demonstration

long enough for me to hope.

Hope this is it,

where I get what's mine

that has been a long time coming

and for the first time I ain't running from it.

BRING IT

Bring it.
I'll tame it
And never lay claim to it.
On some different shit
that's loud
with my feet on the ground
and my head in the clouds

KARMA

One of these days when you least expect
you will know karma,
when you do....
you will think of me.

MY HAPPY PLACE

Imagine pretty flowers in a valley
by a brook
carrying little fish

that kiss the pebbles

and more pretty flowers

in a valley

by the hills

touching the sky

that provides a backdrop

for the scene and

more pretty flowers

in a valley

weighed down with dew dropping

to the earth to be soaked

into the soil

that provides foundation and

more pretty flowers

in a valley

tucked away in a bush

peeping out at me and

more pretty flowers

in a valley

under bare feet that skip attached

to limbs

that reach to the sky

where by and by

life lives and

where off in the distance you can see even more
pretty flowers in the valley waving from below.

MOVEMENT

Although my body is weary,
my mind is alert.
My soul bursts forward
in spurts.
I remind myself
that there is a purpose to my strife,
in my effort
to move on in this life.
Tears threaten to overflow.
Sorrow wants to take charge.
The load on my back
is much too large.
The Queen in me pushes on,
even though my spirit is torn.
I want to be alone,
but it is too quiet there.
I want to walk away,
but I still care.
I must not procrastinate,

or it will be too late.
I must do what needs to be done
or no new wars will be won.

REMEMBER ME

When I cease to be
there will be nothing left of me…
except memories…
if you remember me.
When my world dies
and my light fades away…
the day before I've seen my last day…
there will be nothing more
that I can say except,
"Remember me."
I won't take time to cry
or say good-bye…
I'll want you to remember the life in my eyes
and the close ties…
I've stretched out to each and every one I made contact with…
showering them with my gift of light
and possible insight.
When my pulse dies

and my soul rises

and time flies past me,

I'll whisper in your ear,

"Rejoice!

remember…

my tears flow no longer

and my pain…

is not even a memory."

My suffering will not have been in vain.

I'll have molded an invisible chain of strength.

I'll have faced my demons and won.

I'll have reconnected with the sun

and the moon.

I'll be within the air

you take for granted

and consume.

I'll be that sparkle in the sky

you mistake for a star…

I'll never be far from where you are.

I'll consume the rain

and shower you with my left-over tears

until they are completely depleted.

And that rainbow that leads to never land

will be the place upon which I stand

as you marvel at the suns rays…

not realizing they represent all my yesterdays

because there will be no more tomorrows for me…

remember me

SHIT HAPPENS

Water in the bowl swirls,

representing the world

when its spins and flushes.

Spitting shit back out…

then clearing the way for more…..

 Piss, shit…flush…once more

….That bowl could never be clean.

Piss…

shit…

flush…

once more.

The food made them sick,

they had a stomach flu…

Even worse than…

piss…

shit….

Call Earl….

Flush....

once more.

Have you ever flushed anything you wanted on purpose?

But they say the bowl swirls like the world....

and shit happens all the time.

THE MAKINGS OF YOU

Going through oceans of emotions...

violently shaking me...

overtaking me

with streams of dreams...

that leave tears

and smiles masquerading fears.

For years I've maintained the game...

hiding shame.

Quiet moments give way to my grief...

stealing my joy

...the thief.

Why has so much befallen me?

Yet I stand as trees...

trying not to grieve.

I roll up my sleeves

and fight the fight for life...

ignoring the knife that continues to turn

and how I mourn the loss

that was taken away

at the cost of my true sanity.

Pain... life's gift to humanity...

and so much vanity that it doesn't make sense...

straddling the fence...

scared to jump off in one direction or the other.

Memories of my mother

and streams of lovers

under covers sewn with regret

and discontentment...

leaving my soul bent.

Social malfunctions

that meet at the junction

where my heart,

soul and mind connect.

Feeling like a reject.

Questioning my own self...

trying to get right, what's left.

Seconds,

minutes,

hours,

and years have passed me by...

with no thought of ever saying good-bye.

Forgetting about the promise of forever

and happiness that never came.

If I could scream forever I would.

I don't see a good enough reason why I should.

It would only exhaust what little energy I have left

after the raping of my soul.

So, I write until my fingers cry out,

"NO MORE!

Let us rest!

Back away from the desk.

Shake it off!

Shake it off!

Get up!

Move on!

There is a new beginning at dawn.

Tonight, get your cry out…

get your hurt out…

let it go.

Don't hang on to pain…

it's killing you slow…

You gotta let go.

Don't hang on to the pain.

Yesterday you may have lost

but don't forget your gain…
All the hurt
and pain that you went through,
an old friend once told me,
are the makings of you."
I heard them.

TAKE A MINUTE

Take a minute…
 Realize your mind…
Treasures to find…
Thoughts run deep…
Take a minute…
to leap into life
as it unfolds.
The mind forms a mold of all things…
Good and fair…
Warnings to beware.
Eyes see reality
as the heart continues to pump away…
Carrying your spirit into the next day.
Take a second to reflect on all the things you tend to neglect.
A body that is out of shape trapped inside…

Trying to escape.

Your eyes show a pain that has lasted for years.

Your cheeks leave an invisible trail of tears.

Your hands are moist…

with anticipation.

You can't calm your soul.

You experience frustration.

Your breath smells of stale cigarettes…

you smoke a pack a day to numb the regret.

Take a minute to get a good glance…

Now…

take a second…to chance.

THE RING

I imagined a ring that could bring all things because it caused the power of invisibility and vulnerability:

"The ring that brings all things considered nothing and everything, with no real way of knowing what not showing will bring. It entices desires that are suddenly attainable by ill-gotten means that unstitch the seams of privacy.

Taking liberties because they are free could be seen as the key to advancement or the enhancement of a selfish mind that finds victory in deceit. There is no getting back or going back to a time that has passed, so I ask myself, "When would enough be enough?"

In possession of this ring that brings all things my mind imagines; I am powerful and weak. The wants, craves and desires that fuel my fire have faded in the background of undeserving gifts that are afforded to me at the cost of my dignity, having been reduced to the title of thief. Having it all, I want for nothing and everything, looking forward to nothing because all things are but a mere turn of the ring away. Desire moves. With nothing to look forward to and being in control of it all, growth is not stunted because there is no growth at all. If I could see you, but you couldn't see me, there could be no reflection

Taking is the gift of humanity and so much vanity that it doesn't even make sense. Existing in the midst of battered souls that don't control their own thinking, the ring could be a weapon that could be a blessing. But by my way of thinking, it will only corrupt the already corrupt system that I'm caught up in as I contend with sins of my own. If I could snap my finger and put everything right, the next moment, something would go wrong. The future is unseen, unknown, and attainable. So, this fixation with the ring could last forever and would probably never stop until the ring was stolen, lost, or destroyed. It wouldn't cost me anything except for what I deserve. I could justify and make excuses for all the uses of the ring. I could work out all kinds of ways and things to justify the gifts the ring brings me. I could run with it for a minute and be all caught up in it. In the end, it is exactly what it is:

I'll have gotten rich by an eavesdropping sneaky bitch that sits in the shadow watching.

This paper has me sitting here thinking, "Somebody's here watching that I can't see." Now, the shoe on the other foot is salt in my already open wound that is already infected with bacteria and disease. It's got me looking around more than I usually do. Something has always been watching.

The words read and willed cannot conceal the truth that's hidden, waiting to be reunited with the ones that never run from evolution, the solution to being, not seeing deceitfully or being indiscreetly invisible. Use of the ring is a violation in this: the already crocked game I call living. Time has proven time and time again that advantage is a disadvantage to some: Power spins out of control on some levels, not necessarily in the hand of its beholder.

But then, "If I wasn't supposed to use it…why is it here?" I could toss the question back and forth/forth and back, never changing the fact that I don't care for unknown shadows watching. Basically, if I could, then she probably would, and he probably already has and/or is. Here we have an awakening: It's too much to imagine that all this time, the shadow truly has been watching and truly is whispering and truly isn't me and holds the key, the ring that brings all things to sight unseen.

Getting right down to it, I don't think I'd use it because I know the way my mind works wonders and wanders. I'd think of a way to make a difference so that at the end of the day, I could see my reflection clear and not hear the voices and entertain the notion of being watched all the time, which I'm sure would drive me out of my mind and render me clueless because I'd always wonder who else had a ring. I wouldn't want that kind of pressure cause pressure can burst a pipe. My foundation requires clarity and understanding, breeding insight, and the ease of minds. The want to know is the medicine needed to sustain self in positions producing movement. Use of the ring on any level slants and blurs reality. Then there is this issue of reality and if it's even real. I think I'm awake, but what is thought? To hear me tell it,

"it's the reformation of a dream, producing ideas and arousing sensations that lead in one way or another to what presents as awakening."

What if I had these "real good" ideas? What if I had the ring that brings all things and settles all unsettled shit? What if the ring was meant to fit the finger on my hand because I command my mind and find all pure things to

74

desire, and doing right inspires me? What if inspiration, the will to go, took precedence over the possibility of a shadow lingering in my midst…that might not even exist, and if it did…could be dealt with? Could I resist the opportunity to right wrongs and get back what belongs to us? Could I trust myself to not get out of control and allow the ring to hold me in a position where I mask greed with justification and rationalization?

OR

When you look out the window do you see what I see?
Or do we see two separate realities?
Are we on the same page in this book?
Do we look in the same direction when someone yells, "look?"
 When I reach for your hand do you pull away?
When I say go… Do you stay?
When we are apart…
can you see only me?
Or do you see two…
or three
When I am insecure…
do you make it all better?
Or are you off writing some other love a love letter?
If I understand why I feel the way that I do…

Why can't you see that it's because of you?

THE WHEELS

The wheels are turning really fast,

with no particular destination.

Since there is no oil,

the wheels, in motion, are noisy.

Around and around,

they go, in an unchanging pattern.

Over and under, the wheels will take me

wherever I allow them to.

Sometimes the wheels go so fast

that I can hardly catch up.

The wheels are turning really fast.

Is there some unknown destination…

That only the wheels know of?

I wish that there was oil

for these noisy wheels of mine.

These noisy wheels of mine…

they turn and turn and turn.

THE VISUAL

The visual in my mind, betrays the heart, changing light to dark. Looking into your eyes, seeing no trace of the face I should see. No longer is there a reflection of me. I'm always wondering if you are with someone else while you keep my heart on the highest shelf. You collect numbers and, I fear, give my love away for free...Yet you expect me to feel love and security? My mind races, my fire is wild. All the while, I carry your child. You act as though all is well...like I can simply cast a spell and forget this weight you've put on my back. You expect to be given slack. Filled with silent rage mixed with hate...Have you sealed your fate? I worry, that I won't make it through this storm. In the visual in my mind...I see a swarm that's eating away at my flesh causing an awful bloody mess...Then there you are with bloody lips looking pitiful as you sip. You are so sorry for all this pain brought on by only you and then as if on cue... You tell me that it's my fault...I made you do this deed... It's my fault...that it is your nature to lie and be filled with greed. You always have the saddest story...always a good excuse for your abuse. As my body lay torn apart you sip the blood from my heart... all the while your eyes are alert...Perhaps, searching for another part of me to hurt. It is clear that you don't understand the severity of my sorrow. Happiness is something that I just can't borrow... cause if it ain't real... I can't fake the funk to feel. Each time it's almost done you throw something else in the pot, causing shit to boil to get steamy hot. You run around hugging on bitches collecting numbers to call…and right now I ain't feeling you…at all. Pain in my belly out of control. Taking pills and shots to keep down the food and water that my belly refuses to hold. Eyes all red… cheeks stained with tears. Your lies… all I hear. Heart beating fast with frustration. No sense of happiness or elation. Making all these plans for a future that looks bleak to me…ignoring reality. I can't get a pulse, my heart is put away in a vault and when I look at you I'm thinking "It's all your fault." Now…look at this depressing shit I've been reduced to write. Four hours a sleep a night. You lay snoring at peace with your deception, spreading your lies like infections. Understanding this reality… Is it wise… for you to underestimate me?

LEARNING TO LOVE ME

I tricked myself into thinking that love could genuinely be…
one that binds my heart to yours…
one that binds you to me.
When the darkness came,
I attempted to see the light with all my might…
In the end, you showed your spots…
the snake that you can be.
In doing so…

you showed me that I could be free.

I'm a stronger person because of the pain I went through…

a pain brought on by you.

My heart is stronger.

My mind is alert. I no longer feel beneath the dirt.

Free to love.

Free to see.

I need to be loved for me.

After this, I know one thing to be true…

There is

no love left here…Just pity for you.

My life is turning full circle…

reality helps me see that there could be no love between us

because I had to learn to love me.

ALONE

I'm used to being home alone,

with not even the comforts of a friend or phone

talking softly to my own self

examining what's left of the one love that I thought was true.

A love shared by me and you.

You say you don't mean to hurt me…

But you do.

I never imagined these things of you.

For the first time,

I am unable to let shit slide

I will not simply come along for the ride.

I need more.

This is not the way I plan to live,

with more pain than love to give.

SALTY TEARS

No windows for a view,

no doors to leave,

trapped inside,

I grieve.

No one knows where I live,

with more pain than joy to give.

The grass died long ago,

not from people walking to and fro,

but, because there is no sun here, no rain…

just salty tears.

THE WEED YOU PLANTED

The seed you planted yesterday

has grown a little more today.

The roots have spread, and the dew is gone,

a weed sprouted up today.

Oh, how I hate for a weed to grow,

for all it will do is spread.

You can mow it, spray it, even burn it…

but, a weed is never quite dead.

This weeds you planted in my yard.

You can put back where it came.

But when it's gone

this yard of mine

will never be the same.

I'll always remember that weed of yours

and how you let it grow.

You better be sure that weed of yours

is not the reason I let you go.

I trusted you to water the grass

and tend it with love

and for a while

it was a beautiful lawn,

as though sent from heaven above.

When my eyes were looking the other way

you quietly slipped in your weed.

Then claimed to not know where it came from.

Now what kind of shit are you trying to feed me

the one who knows you both inside and out,

the one who knows

what you're really about,

the one who trusted you with everything she holds dear,

then you slipped in your weed,

the one thing

I most fear.

JUICE

The juice in this cup...

overflows no more.

Its taste?

Rotten to the core.

Its color?

Faded.

Shelf life?

Traded for one more sweet.

Because this juice

smells of sour feet

that stomped and stomped...

making the juices flow

through moist and dirty toes...

that spoiled its taste…

making all that stomping a waste.

Its smell is foul…

though the grapes grew for miles

in a field of bull shit…

its flavor…

smell

and taste?…

are all unfit.

DID I FLASH?

When you hurt my heart and even made me cry…

even said good-bye…

Did I flash like you did?

When you did things that drove my brother away…

I still don't see him this very day…

Did I flash like you did?

Collecting numbers,

telling lie after lie,

coming up with fake alibis.

Did I flash like you did?

Calling me names,

treating my heart like a game,

Did I flash like you did?

While I held your baby near

you took a stance,

causing me to fear,

on a day that was otherwise clear,

causing me to flash,

bringing back memories from my past.

I saw in you what I saw in him.

Clear skies are gone.

The sky is grim.

INURED HEART #1

Injured heart

will not heal,

throbbing pain,

all I feel…

tortured soul…

bottomless pit…

pieces that just won't fit…

exhausted eyes

can't shed a tear,

the future unclear.

Faded smile lingers on.

Life?

Where is your charm?

Postures don't look too strong.

My step is all wrong.

My feet walked too many miles.

Defeat ain't my style.

Hope?

There is a trace.

The past can't be erased.

Looking back?

Why to see myself cry?

There is movement ahead.

My soul ain't dead.

Run away?

Who me?

Ain't no pain gon ever beat me.

INJURED HEART #2

Devil...

can't claim this.

Life...

may not be bliss.

Rearrange...

Push on.

I could never be alone.

I can't hide,

The Creator is by my side

sharing this here load,

taking control,

healing my heart.

Hope?

A new start,

freedom is near

The past is

where I put the tears.

Pain can't be my friend.

Crying does not have to be my trend.

I'm alive

not dead

with some roads ahead.

I'll face them all.

It will never be said that I fled.

INJURED HEART #3

Judgment...

was not your chance to do as you please...

break me down at the knees…

thinking…I'd beg… please, please…

your love was a tease.

You thought…

then explained it away…

thinking you would live to fight another day…

Your face has no trace just empty space.

Your silence is cold,

waiting for me to unfold,

and break this here mold that has always been mine.

Putting dust where I shine.

My emotions decline.

Me?

Share this space with such an empty face

like a drug laced with deception, empty eyes, lies and alibis?

What?

THE MOOD OF MAY

I want to tell you something…

My world is in a mess

and must confess to being the cause of it all.

I have been living on hope for a little too long now.

I've slowed all the way down now

and it's really starting to eat at me.

It's nibbling every inch of me and I

can feel it and see it and know it and still I stay still.

I told myself I was waiting on a sign

and didn't realize that it would be the same sign

as last time all over again.

Sitting right here

I can see every bit of me

and I could beat the shit outta me

if I didn't think that this is all a part of the test

that my soul only recently started to study for.

Time does have its way with me.

To be able to see so clearly

that each time the light nearly shined in the end…

I blocked it.

And the shit has gotten detrimental…

no bull shittin…

it's fundamentally the truth.

I've withdrawn into myself on purpose again

and can't pretend otherwise.

Starting over again is getting old again.

And I'm ready to settle into that groove that moves me.

I feel it in my bones not letting me be alone

so, all I can do is move and stand still at will

and recognize the patterns

and signs that radiate or block shine.

I feel the change in the wind that begins each of my capers that

allowed me to put it down on paper and right now it's telling me

to "come on!"

HERE I SIT

Here I sit with thoughts running through my mind,

looking for what I need to find,

hoping all is well,

looking for a needle that fell.

I'm looking for a diamond

in a bucket filled with cracked glass,

I'm looking for an earring in the grass,

looking for a ribbon that landed in the mud…

I'm trying to save my soul from the flood.

I can find one shoe,

but can't find the other. I'm

looking for my mother in my brother.

Trying to find that clasp that fell from around my neck.

It fell through that crack in the deck.

looking for the car.

Where did I park?

looking for the light in the dark.

Looking for hope,

where there appears to be none.

My cake is burning,

it's long past done.

Where is my remote?

I don't want to watch this.

There goes that bus I missed.

Where is the cab, I called three hours ago?

Traffics moving way to slow.

Here I sit, trying to get myself together.

The weatherman told lied,

look at this weather.

Where are my cards?

I want to play solitaire…

I looked where I put them,

they are not there looked for quiet,

 the noise was too loud. looked for the sun…

All I saw were clouds.

I wanted the rain to grow my plants.

Trying to get up. I can't.

Where is my friend?

faded into the night…

looking for what was right

found what was wrong.

Tried to fix it.

But it took too long.

Frustrated,

can't call this feeling fear.

until I figure it out,

Imma sit here

watch time past,

see how long this stretch will last.

Looked for the sun looked for a smile

it would be nice at least once in a while

GHOST CREATION

If the ghost sits in the corner,

it can see every bit of me

uninhibited and free…

in my nature.

It can see my thoughts,

feel my heart,

knows that I am caught here,

knows that I am sincere

and that things are not as they appear all the time.

It finds me wandering in a place far,

far away rooted to a day

in all of my dreams

that seems to drain me

but really sustains me in this place

I'm forced to undergo,

where I know the deal,

where I feel deeply

when the ghost reaches out

just as I'm about to slip away in a dream.

For just a moment I pause.

I look around and wait to see if he'll let me see him.

I talk to the old lady that is sometimes here.

I make it clear that she can stay

and that we can chill into the next day

unless she gets to tripping.

She respects me

because she can see that she is safe here with me.

Her ghost remains though

I've never restrained her.

When the wind chimes blew I

knew

that others were waiting too.

One plays with words,

One writes them down,

One hears rhythm in every sound,

One marvels over paint,

One plays with a brush,

One dives into a project with a lover's lust,

One is a daydreamer

all of the time,

One takes to the stage

and shines,

One can tell stories,

One can hear.

One can see,

One knows no fear,

One is a philosopher to the bone...

They are all far from home,

all live deep in my heart and dome,

they set the pace they set the tone

in my world in my home.

They represent the one you see

when you look directly at me.

Sometimes when I am out and about

I feel energies so strong

that I hold on to my composure

and I can't get close to people

without shaking because the energy is taking its toll

on the little soul name Robin

that lay sobbing

most of the time

because of the crime called living

where all that is really given and taken is time...

I'm tired

STABILITY

I'm not lazy.

I am skilled at all I do.

I'm a good worker

when I work.

It's like all I can commit to is this writing,

which stays consistently inviting me on a regular basis

in spells.

At work I go through the motions,

consciously insulted by the fact that I am there

instead of here.

It's a problem.

It's not even like I don't understand.

I see the shit keeps coming.

I'm here at the last minute before actions must be taken.

Right here I sit and sat and saw this it coming.

It's a problem.

Somehow, I know that it will all come together

but still have the sense to be one half step from pure panic.

Me and panic can't get along

and I unravel on levels in my mind

that make me hibernate

9 out of 12 months in a year.

I am calming myself down right now

before I close my eyes to sleep.

I feel my heart race because

I know I am about to pop.

I can feel it all around me it has gotten real bad here lately.

It's got me being a prisoner in my home afraid of the outside.

It's got me beautifying my space.

It's got me watching me do this shit.

Today I tried harder than the day before

to just maintain self…

just to open the front door.

It's hard because I am a mother.

Mentally I sometimes feel unstable.

I need …help me.

I am the light that shines and the cloud that hides.

I am all things held together.

For me It's about getting some momentum

and keeping it going

and all the while remain interested and aware.

Aware that shit accumulates

while people meditate.

I'm gonna concentrate real hard

and ask for strength to get back up in the morning.

It might not happen in one day but tomorrow

I will start getting things back together.

The gap isn't so wide that it cannot be fixed.

I can get it together again.

Then I will read these words one day

and remember when I actively decided to pursue stability.

THE HEALING PROCESS

Veins filled with tears,

sting every part of my being.

I'm drowning.

My tears rip out of me

like pages from a book.

As hard as I try,

they will not subside.

My soul is hurting.

My heart aches.

My mind…

it's racing.

This pain…

is bigger than anything that I have ever known.

I'm so alone, inside myself.

There seems to be nothing left on the shelf.

I ask the Creator to have mercy.

Forgive me.

Take this pain that consumes me,

that has the power to sneak up on me and steal my joy.

Replace it with peace of mind.

Allow my mind to rest.

I feel as though I will explode.

These emotions take control.

They have me stuck, stifled.

I want to run. I want to hide.

These are not options.

I'm sick with grief.

There is no sign of relief.

I can't do this anymore.

The salt burns me to the core.

They tell me to get over it, to move on.

How can I explain that my feet refuse to move?

I'm trying to make sense of this mess.

I'm trying to

understand.

I'm afraid.

I'm afraid of repeating the past.

The issues started a long time ago.

There was a lack of mother's love.

I didn't always feel it.

So I settled for whatever.

Here I sit…

again…

contending with emotions

that threaten to overtake me. I

don't like this…

On second thought…

My children…My children.

They are the purpose of my strife,

striving to give them a better life…

than mine.

I'm so afraid.

My tears flow in a non-stop fashion.

Burning my eyes…

Burning my eyes.

If I could…

I would stop them…

Stop the pain, stop the tears,

stop the confusion,

stop the illusion, stop the sadness,

and stop the madness.

But they flow, the rivers I cry…they flow.

Maybe it's all a part of the healing process.

Understanding

this, when will I be healed?

REMIND MYSELF

Toy told me to write about this shit so that I could release it. I
told her I had over 600 pages, none of which set stages to even
begin to dive into the evil connected to this string she was telling
me to pull. I told he that some buttons were not meant to be
pushed and some pages should not be turned. I told her that I
could light a match, toss gasoline, and watch that mutha fucka
slow burn…even turn him. I told her that I could start at his
forehead and work my way all the way down the middle to his
insides and watch the mutha fucka bleed and it still would not
impede the hate that feeds me. I told her that I should not start a
topic that I can't control when it comes to taking souls. He is a
child molester. What the fuck else am I supposed to write. The
judicial system could never make him pay enough so I dream to
watch him die at night. I dream to see him dangle at an angle

where he can see that it's me who snaps the thread. That it's me who could see him dead. I have to remember to tell Toy that she is speaking on some shit she knows nothing about.

MUTHA FUCKA

I pegged you to be lazy,

demanding,

obsessive,

to lie,

to be a pothead,

mentally abusive,

withdrawn,

afraid,

insincere,

self-absorbed,

talented,

closed-minded,

stern,

jealous,

Crooked

have lots of issues,

to be angry,

unmotivated,

immature,

evil,

Lazy

untrustworthy,

unreliable,

wasteful,

without a business mind,

unprepared,

a procrastinator,

a masturbator,

a manipulator,

a control freak,

to be afraid to grow,

to be insincere in my growth,

to be sad and to be hostile.

I just didn't peg you to be a child molester.

With all the things I pegged you for…

How did I miss that?

GOOD ENOUGH

I was good enough to sleep with,

though you barely knew my name.

I was good enough to comfort,

any time you thought I felt pain.

I was good enough to lecture,

any time you thought I'd lost my way.

I was good enough to wait for...

yet

another day.

I was good enough to confide in.

I was good enough to trust.

I was good enough to be lavished

with all your lust.

I was good enough to laugh with,

even good enough to cry.

I was good enough that

you never wanted to hear me say good- bye.

I was good enough to give you

this little bundle of life,

But you're not ready

to say that I'm good enough...

to be your wife?

The fact that you feel this way

cuts me like a knife.

One day you may want me...

and

I will no longer want to be

your wife.

A FACT

If it were not for my children
and worrying about their strife,
I swear to God
I'd take his good for nothing life.

JUST BE

I blink the tears that will not fall.
My heart calls out.
My mind understands.
I blink the tears that will not fall.
My heart calls out.
My mind understands.
I sit still and wait
thinking of food I ate
when I wasn't hungry.
Chin in hand,
I now understand the cycle.
I blink the tears that will not fall
when all I want to do is cry.

I don't want to question why.

I just want to cry.

I want the tears to fall

and when they are done

I want it all to be over.

I want to begin again,

with a plan in hand to remain and

not be restrained.

I sit alone in my home consumed

with peace that sits in discord.

Battling the notion of the Lord,

Creator or God.

It's hard for me to just believe so I grieve.

My mind will not let it be…

the questions that reside in me.

I wonder if I had unconditional faith if my plate would be less
full.

I pull answers put of the air. Everywhere

I am I am separate,

never connected...

always conflicted

and naturally reflective all the time.

I find myself outside of me

and I wonder what it must be like to just be.

PICKING UP THE PIECES

Scattered on the floor in a million pieces,

lay my life.

I'm careful not to step on the pieces.

Some of them appear to be missing.

I kneel with a bag collecting them all.

They fill the bag completely.

The weight ruptures the bottom...

The pieces fall again onto the cold floor,

this time...

shattering them into even smaller,

sharper,

pieces,

causing my fingers to be cut.

The sharp pieces plant themselves in the bottom of my feet,

causing me to bleed,

causing me to hurt all

over again.

THE RAMBLING OF A MIND

I have much disdain for mundane sameness,

bane of real existence,

where resistance seems futile

and meanwhile the cycle goes on.

I question this very moment in time

that rhymes with yesterday

and fight to stay on the outside

rather than ride the roller coaster

that ends in the same place.

All I really know is what they say,

and I don't even know who they are.

I'm talking about a time that none of us,

to my knowledge

lived in..if it even existed.

The masses in flock embraced information at some point

and that information was passed down

and rearranged like a whisper passed down a line

 and what remains are the restraints

put in place for one purpose or another,

purpose being something that breeds movement.

So, from a distance it looks like activity.

Up close it looks like restraints.

Seeing with all of my eyes open

I see so many closed,

the cause for my pause and cause.

Quiet moments entice me and invite me in.

I stay a while and lay down crumbs that will lead the others.

Suspended in time,

a normal routine in the cycle,

knowing that it goes one way or the other

and there are still possibilities

that I have not yet entertained,

I remain seeing and agonizing

over the senselessness of the relentless pattern

that holds me captured.

The struggle swells like the mouse

moving through the snake.

It encompasses and smothers,

taking life worth living,

giving way to deep seeded despair.

Imagine being the beam of sunshine on the inside

that cries out and rebels.

If causality is the root

then everything causes something

and something causes everything.

Does life bring death

and what does death cause?

I can't call it cause

I don't know and neither does anyone else.

If every action causes a reaction,

then what caused the action to react.

What about the actions that no one knows what the reaction is

because they are on the other side of a line

that no one has seen to cross?

All I really know is what people say

and have been saying with no foundation except hope,

a deep-seated longing based on desire.

Fueled with the fire based on what?

Going off instinct

I stand paused at the mere concept of death.

Life is a given.

Time is all we have

because when time is gone

no one knows what's next,

making time, itself, the currency of the universe.

Everybody has some

and everything takes some.

Does time go on forever?

I can't ever remember never not being and not seeing.

At some point I had to have arrived.

Before that, where was I?

Sanity?

What is sane?

And who made that word up?

Who decided on the half full and a half empty cup?

Inkblots look like all kinds of spots to me,

kind of like clouds you see?

I sit here knowing the essence of me

and it's frightening.

My mind really does travel

and I know how to be real still.

A part of the cycle is to keep beginning again

in one way or another

and never catch up.

It is advancement each time I notice it.

Knowing could never be enough.

Action is required.

I remember tripping on sleep.

I spend as much time asleep as I do awake

if not more.

I am itching to get a peep at sleep

and what it really is.

That's a lot of unaccounted for time.

If you take away the body what, if anything, is left?

Have you ever seen a soul?

Have you ever felt a soul?

In the center of my eyes I see souls controlling moments

that carry and all of them are not smiling.

The energy they give of makes me cold.

If words are what we speak and we speak their language,

compiled of words they created, is it not possible that our

thinking is limited to their vocabulary?

How can you label a sensation that cannot be accurately defined?

Each person feels and responds to a sensation differently.

We are born with senses not language.

We mimic "ma ma" and "da da",

some say its universal,

I say it's because that's what we hear over and over again.

Then we are introduced to vocabulary

that labels things like chairs, books…tangible things.

The inventors of words went so far

as to even label most other things that cannot be held.

Most people can hear, taste, smell, feel and see.

So, they labeled these senses.

Most people get angry, love, hate and care.

Those words are filed away under the emotions category.

They have a category for everything.

They started with the number one

and went as far as they could,

must have got tired of coming up with more words for numbers

so, they made up the word infinite.

Every now and then they throw another word in the dictionary.

Just to make sure no one gets confused

they came up with the thesaurus,

a book that gave you words

to take the place of words that you commonly use.

What if we didn't have words?

What if telepathy is real...

only the insertion of words weakened our abilities

and somewhere in that supposedly unused part of our brain

lays the lock,

only we don't remember the combination

because all we can remember are the words?

If you label it

people will stretch the definition to suit their end.

Say what you like,

but like what you say.

I sometimes find myself in predicaments that I didn't see coming

until they were there

and then when I sit back and reflect,

I see I knew it all along.

This self-fulfilling prophecy shit they talk about

really does exist.

Careful what you put in the midst,

and Karma? That shit is real too.

Personally witnessed hindsight shows it to be true.

PIT BULL LOVER

I'm Blue in a cage, let out in a corner
feeling trapped in the pit of my pit bull heart
could tear apart some shit
while the outsiders think they running it.
I'll swing, I'll swing with a force
bound to connect, from behind your back,
 grab your face, miss and snap your neck
behind disrespect from your lips,
now watch me flip the script and loose grip.
Now look what you done did,
Done fucked with the kid who ain't playin wit cha,
ain't shit like you…
Do what the fuck I do then stroll out.
Think first or be about rehearsal…you and a slow ride to the
cemetery…
It's scary how far I can take it…
but you make it so easy.

TO ALL OF YOU

To all of you who took from me,

"How dare you disrespect me so carelessly and thoughtlessly?

You've eaten bits and pieces of my heart,

leaving me torn in moments, hours, days, weeks, and years.

I woke up this morning…I said I woke up this morning

clearly seeing your storm of potential and existing harm to my

being.

I woke up seeing clearly.

It hurt my feelings so bad

after I got past my initial hopes that dimmed to disbelief

then to realization then disappointment then anger.

Anger laces my hurt feelings. So, to all of you, "tread lightly."

CHAPTER FOUR / Being a Fool

I was all over the place. I was popping pills like they were going
out of style. Each month a different drug was introduced because
the last one was not doing what it was supposed to do. I didn't
like the medicine head sensation that comes from taking anti-
depressants. I remember taking the boys to get a haircut. I must
have been deep in thought because I suddenly realized that one
of the barbers was waving his hand in front of my eyes, trying to
see if I could see. I was highly medicated and was walking
around feeling dazed all the time. Some people like the feeling of

being high all the time—I am not one of those people. I need at least a semblance of control. I decided not to take the pills anymore. I thought I felt better, so I stopped going to therapy. I told myself if I ever needed it, at least I knew I would go. Even with the help of therapy, that period of my life is foggy. I remember finding myself again. I remember realizing that I was a painter. I remember loving my natural hair. I'd never worn it natural before. With Van in jail, I felt new and improved. Life eventually settled down again.

I recognize people who can't "not" be in a relationship because I was once one of those people. I remember my first encounter with Miguel like it was yesterday. I went to a cookout with one of my girlfriends. I can't remember whose house it was. I remember Miguel though. He was a tall, dark Mandingo warrior-type brother with a deep voice that relaxed every part of my being. At the time, he somehow reminded me of a tall chocolate Tupac. He came and sat beside me, smelling all good, and asked if I was there alone. I'm a mess when I want to be, so the rest is history. At first, Miguel was like a dream come true. He was so into me that it made no sense at all. I met his mom and brother. We even got engaged. I was going to have my normal family. Miguel caught me at a time in my life when I needed a connection. He could have told me the grass was blue, and the sky was green, and I would have believed him. Miquel was the type of brother that needed a lot. He needed shelter, a ride, motivation, a couple of dollars, my keys, you name it, he needed it. Miguel didn't call me "mommy" for no reason. Now and again, he would work, and it seemed like he finally got his head on straight. It never lasted though. Miguel drove me to work in my BMW every day and was there to pick me up on time like clockwork, and I was so proud. You couldn't tell me nothing. I'll never forget that time I was at work. My cubicle was by a window.... on the first floor. Why I look up and see Miguel outside the window watching. I was so embarrassed. I was like, "What the hell...what are you doing?"

The problem with Miquel was simple. He was a mean-spirited alcoholic who always had a red cup and a brown bag. To make matters worse, he didn't trust women. He thought every woman was just like the last woman who had done him wrong. In his eyes, every woman was a cheater and a whore. No matter how much love I showed him, he could never get past what that last woman did. He was jealous to the core. Miguel would lose his mind if we went out and another man held the door open for me. It got to the point where I didn't want to go places with him. When we were in the car, I had to either look straight at him or straight ahead. If my eyes took in another soul, he would go off on one of his tangents about how I was looking at another man. By this time, I was too far into him. I had moved him in. He bought a dog and everything. We planted trees on the lawn, and we were the perfect couple to eyes that didn't know any better. Miguel left with my car one night and did not return until the following day. I was livid. But not enough to not let him drive me to work in my car and keep it for the day. Yes, I can spot a fool because I've been a fool.

By this time, I was a part of a poetry troop called "Lotus Stage Tapestry." Interesting story. I've always written poetry. It never dawned on me to recite it. My friend Toy suggested that I try out for a poetry troop. I mustered up the courage to do it. The lady in charge asked all the people auditioning to go to their own area and write about "Elders." I found a spot and went to work writing the first thing that came to my mind about elders. After some time had passed, the lady had us all line up. I was last. I didn't know what was happening or what to expect. Turns out, now we all had to go on stage and read out thoughts on elders. Everybody was writing about grandmamas and aunties. I was at the end of the line, panicking because I had taken a different route with my thinking. When I thought of the word "Elders," I automatically thought of myself levitating. I thought of people all around me levitating too. Before I knew it, it was my turn. By now, it was a wet tissue in my hands. I was sweating bullets. So I took a deep breath and said,

"Soulfully I submit, opening myself wide for scrutiny and growth, seeing possibilities that are normally overlooked. Taking the sun with me...radiating...exploding with inner peace. At one with myself...Realizing, understanding, and learning lessons promptly, moving on ahead...loving me all the way. Sharing and caring and loving freely and honestly.

The rivers are subsiding, no longer dividing my soul from my heart. Looking out, I see destruction. I hear warning bells that echo silently, warning a few but...not the masses. Justice or lack of justice...is commonplace in this place I've been forced to call home and forced to endure, like a disease with no cure...How can they make pure when they are not pure...but we are?

I soulfully surrender to the cause of my people to do its deeds and fill its needs to plenty. I humbly accept my path to correction, although I possess no sense of direction... I'll walk blindly...seeing a different perspective. I open my mind to give it fresh air and to see what's in there. Images so vivid control the tone...pounding at my dome, wondering again and again. But in the midst, I touched a soul, told it to take control, told it that it didn't need to be meek, told it to see its potential from the inside with no hindrance from the outside...then decide...being selective.

Realizing my own mind...I could feel it like the soft touch of my
love...extending completely and holding on. I touched a soul this
week with words that others would not speak...but I did.
I unflinchingly lay my life on the line to protect what's mine all
the time because little things mean so much and go so far to
distant stars, stirring laughter and smiles, cementing...bonding
positive energy...potential reality...turning the key...showing the
universe that we can detach our mind from ourselves long
enough to see the view...off in the distance...yet ever so near.
Flow freely with your thoughts. Catch your thoughts in midair.
Adore each concept...Question each point and realize that it
always leads back to what is paramount...Soulfully I
submit...opening myself wide...for scrutiny and growth.

I made the troop. We rehearsed on weekends. Miguel hated it.
He just knew that one of those "poet people" was trying to take
his woman. It was my first show. I was so excited. I couldn't
wait for Miguel to hear my new material so he'd see what all the
rehearsals were about. By then, he'd promised that he was not
drinking anymore. Like a fool, I took him at his word. He met
me at the cafe where I was performing. I knew something was
off about him. He was sweating bullets. I kept asking him if he
was okay. He said he was. About that time, it started to rain. I
asked him to run to my car and roll my window up. He obliged.
The fact that he never came back in bothered me because he had

my keys. When the event was over, I walked to my car to find Miguel locked inside and passed out while holding a big red cup containing Henny and coke. I knocked and knocked on the window. This fool was dead to the world. He finally got himself together long enough to open the window. I had never been so embarrassed. It became clear that he had a severe drinking problem.

Things went downhill from there. The last straw for me was when he started driving a different car. He told me that the vehicle belonged to his mother. We went everywhere in that car. One night we drove my car to his mom's house for something. I stayed in the car. I noticed the car he drove me around in, pulling up beside me. A very unattractive woman got out and went into the house next door to his mother's house. I sat there for a minute, and then being me, I got out of the car, walked up to the door, and knocked on it. The woman came to the door with a visible attitude. I politely asked her whose car she was driving. This bitch looks me dead in the eyes and says,

"You need to ask your man that."

Right before I got a chance to snatch her up by her throat, Miguel came running out, looking alarmed. When he started to stutter, I knew he was fixing his mouth to lie. He tried to do everything he could to get me off that woman's steps. The lady ran inside her house while talking shit through her door. By then,

I was walking to my car. Miguel's mom came outside, talking about how she didn't want any trouble outside her house. I told her,

"Oh, it's too late."

I reached into my glove compartment and grabbed my switchblade. In my mind, I'd had about all the disrespect I was going to take. I saw red. Miguel was pleading by then,

"Get in the car, Robin! Baby, get in the car!"

I should have cut his ass, but instead, I had my heart set on cutting a brand-new smile on that trash-talking bitch who was laughing at me from behind her door. Miguel made up some lie to cool me off. It was too much for me. I knew it was over, but I had to get him back.

I've always been into herbal remedies. I tend to keep little jars of this and that. Miguel swore up and down that I was spooky. I've never been very religious, so in his small mind, I had to be some witch or something. I used his fears against him. I'm dramatic by pure nature. It was nothing for me to put on all black, gather some powdered incense and some oil, along with a little bag of salt and a little bag of flour. I talked my good friend Licia into going along with me. She dressed in all black, too. I drove to his house and parked. Licia and I had ourselves a good ol-pretend ritual right in front of Miguel's mom's house, where he was staying. I lit some small candles, made a little volcano out of the powdered incense, and poured a little of the scented oil in it, and before I knew it, I was striking a match, and we had a nice little fire going. Just for shits and giggles, I blew flour and salt out of my hand as I pointed to the house. Then I wrapped the candles in a red cloth and slammed them on the ground. After I did all that, Licia and I turned around and around in circles and pointed to Miguel's mom's house, chanting some fake language we made up on the spot. It was hilarious. I remember us getting back in the car and muttering under my breath,

"Stop laughing, Licia Stop laughing!"

I thought we would pee on ourselves as we rode off because we laughed so hard. It was the funniest payback ever. The man next door to Miguel's mother's house was cutting his grass during our "ritual," He stopped dead in his tracks like we placed him in a trance. I knew that if Miguel was not shivering with fear in the window while watching, our act would surely get back to him and the entire neighborhood. To this day, Miguel thinks I threw a curse on him. That's what he gets for playing with fire like it don't burn.

THE ONE

I loved them all…
Akindele,

121

Deleen, David,

Pinner,

Antonio

even Kevin,

but Michael?

He really could have been the one.

He felt just like he was the one,

came right out and said he was the one.

Walked like the one, talked like the one,

sounded like the one, proud like the one,

sexy like the one, stamina like the one,

freaky like the one, sweet like the one,

playful like the one, had cool family like the one,

handled me like the one, did almost everything

just like the one in my mind I'd call my King…

If only he had been who he pretended to be.

 He should have really been My Miguel.

Instead, he was a tall, chocolate, intimidated by knowledge,

mama house loving, deep voice having, affectionate, lying,

justifying mean ass, semi-functioning alcoholic, and my silly ass

still craves his embrace to this day and it's been years.

WHY HAST THOU FORSAKEN ME?

"Love, Love!

Why hast thou forsaken thee and taken thee on this, the most unharmonious ride never to see the brighter side of Love? Why hast thou called thee name in the midst of the rain that breaks souls and controls sense? Why hast thou let thee straddle the fence that divides fantasy from common sense, hence the tragedy that has fast become me?"

"My Child,

this state must require unrest in order for thou to see that the best is yet to arrive and to live not simply survive for false Love or Love that is incomplete and grows obsolete in the line of pure vision that makes provision for healing the weak and fortifying the meek with understanding, demanding action that breeds satisfaction in positive ends and does not pretend to know Love and its meaning. It quails all meaning except truth and allows the view to clear as it pulls thee near to where the light stands, and the rain ends all in the name of self-love."

"Love, Love,

Why must thee cry real tears that burn and yearn for another for years and years? Why must the cover of the night bring sadness and fear in the dawn that lingers on an on even when it is not felt. Why must thou ght with thee to not see the real? Why must thee feel hurt inside and want to hide from all who see? Why hast thou forsaken me?"

"My Child,

I give you sight to see in the cover of night. I shield you from real harm, and my arms are always holding, and the souls are always consoling and controlling the tempo you see as limbo. Each step you take and all you go through are, My Child, the makings of you. Your strength is being fine- tuned and groomed for your forever, and I can't expect you to never question or ponder, but please don't wander from your light. It protects you in the night and the dawn of the day. It will never let you stay on the outside of clarity. It spares turmoil as it toils your soul and pulls your control into range and view. My Child I have never forsaken you."

"Love, Love,

Didn't you feel the Love in my heart when you let us part and allowed me to walk away from the one Love I wanted to stay? Didn't you feel how deep it went for me and how he was meant for me? Didn't you see how the Love had been a long time coming and for the first time I wasn't running? Didn't you see me let him into my life and how I longed to be his wife? Didn't you know that I loved to say his name and see time bring him to me? Love, why hast thou forsaken me?"

My Child,

I feel the pain and strain pulling at your heartstrings. I arrived to bring clarity and the charity of sight. I know you don't think it's right. But you had to see that he was controlling and holding you back. Each time you dabbled, you lost track of your positive end and had to defend your character. I felt how deep it went for you and saw how time was spent wasted as you tasted the bitter truth and suffered the abuse of your soul as you let him control you. I could let you sit and let you stay and play at false forever that may never arrive. But I chose to let you stay and survive with another chance and possibly another. I will not stand idly by and watch him smother you. When you could not see, I could, and that is why it's all to the good when I tell you to, "hush, now Child," and embrace your light and sleep in the blanket of night. Wake to a new day with something else to say besides self-pitying remarks. My Child, I have never forsaken thee. What will it take of me to make you see that today is your birthday the first day to a forever that has never been tampered with, a personal gift from you to you by way of you and life that has had its share of sacrifice and the knife that continued to turn has been burned and can't be felt. The welts from the sting now bring you wisdom and vision if you would just open them wide, the eyes that were born to see and be free, the eyes that feel and reveal concepts that live in the depth of your soul that has never been yours to control. All the wishing will never quail the intuition that was born in you, and the scorn in you was adopted when you opted to look the other way rather than stand and stay in the light. In the back of your mind, you know I'm right. My Child, I have never forsaken thee."

"Love, Love,
What was the point in all that time wasted, and all the bitter pain tasted as I pasted pieces to hold together Love? Why come so close to have to turn back? What did the love lack? Can I fix it? Can I make it right? Can I utilize this light to my positive end can I mend him?"

"My Child, listen."
"I'm listening." "

My Child, look."

"I'm looking."

"My Child,

Do you not see the cycle that has gradually become your idea of Love? Do you not want more for yourself? Had you never encountered a lifetime of pain, do you honestly think you would have evaded strain and gained more Love? Could you be so accustomed to heartache that you don't know how to wait or take care of you?

My Child,

I'm telling you that it's all in and about you and how you view yourself on that shelf far…far away rooted to a day when innocence was lost at the cost of your pure understanding. I can't take you back to make it right, but I can get you through the night and set on a path that is right for you. The hour has come for you to not run or walk. Stand still. Battle the will to go to a place you know breeds confusion and lives in delusion in the form of a nightmare set in place to scare you not dare you to see.

My Child,

you ain't gon worry me. I've got you now and won't let you fall it's time to make sure you don't drop this ball that reeks of success and contentment while you attempt to remain on a relentless path to destruction running from your induction into the realm of being and the land of the seeing that you inherited and are merited for. In you resides the dream maker or dream taker. Which will you allow to prevail? Think my Child, think and come pass the brink to the realm of the seeing…and being.

"But Love,

I miss him?" "My Child,

My Child,

Miss him but love you. Miss him but love you through and through with the understanding that your decision-making process has been made temporarily faulty, so the tears are salty instead of sweet. Fight the defeat that stays and remains and restrains and detains your happiness. You are stronger and have lived longer than you know. The beauty is bound to show because it is real. No amount of confusion will let you stay stagnant or be a magnet for distention and not to mention heartache. Don't be afraid to take this step and be swept away and washed clean to the shore with more than Love to share. Spare yourself the pain as you acknowledge your gain by accepting reality and embracing the clarity you know exists in the midst of all the drama. Stop blaming your mama. Get up and reclaim this half-full cup as your life and make the moves and sacrifices to be. Miss yourself enough to go back and get you on track. Move ahead through and pass the storms out of harm's way to a better day that lives forever and never look back unless you're checking to make sure you've remained on track. It's a fact that life is pain and that there will always be rain and storms, showers, breeding life, flowers, and love. Use your gift or lose your gift and expect to shift to the other side where nothingness lies in waits and can't wait to seal your fate.

My Child,

I am Love. I am you...stop fighting and start inviting better days in the Sun's rays that lift the haze and allows you to see as far as you want to see and be what you were born to be. You've lived forever and can never escape life. You remain the Wife of Time and the Sun that shines by and by. The Sky so blue is every bit of you. See that Love, feel that light, and know that the decision to move on was right. Standing still should never have been a choice. It would have put you standing still instead of running your course.

My, Child

I am so proud to call you mine that's the reason you shine. Shine My Child, Shine."

"Love,

The sorrow stung and brought connecting tears from my heart to my eyes for the first time this time and made me cry briefly. I know the pain is smoldering beneath me and my surface. I am trying to understand what the purpose of the Love was, now questioning if it even exists in the midst of this cruel…cruel world. The numb sensation is expanding in my being, and for the first time I'm seeing Love less clearly, it's nearly gone. All that is left is the storm that is brewing as I sit stewing over the unfairness of it all, questioning if I ever experienced real Love at all. I reflect on yesterday at a love that I longed to stay near me. In the end, it pierces me through and through, and all that's left are memories of the one Love that I just knew to be true. Love was to complete me, not defeat me. I sit in the middle of my living room, and the sadness in my eyes reflects the doom and gloom that perfume the air everywhere. Realizing that letting go was for the best does not prompt me to rest more easily. I miss the companionship and the relationship that was to grow into forever. It never dawned on me that he would take me to the day where I had to leave and wanted to stay at the same time and find a way to make it work until the point where it hurt just to dream the dream that was tearing at my seams and taking my breath and all that is left is questionable memories and a fading dream. I sit daunted and taunted by all the time wasted on a fantasy that was to be a reality in my head. I reflect on the things he said and things he did. I realize that he hid his true nature right in front of my eyes, and I blame myself for trying to make him into a king and believing in a dream that will never come true. My Love was real, though misguided. I decided to dive feet first into the unknown with a man who may be fully grown but is still a boy playing with little boy toys with the devil's ways. That is why he will probably always stay as he is. I probably should not wonder if he is hurting like I am or if he ever really gave a damn or if he was just trying to get over on my back like a bridge to all the tomorrows that he took for granted as he planted the idea of forever as he promised to never leave. He is the source of the reason I grieve because he deceived me into believing in him. All the false promises broke time and again should have let me see the real him, but I chose to stay and stand and wait to adopt a misplaced faith. I'm angry with myself for thinking that all that is

131

left is sadness for not rejoicing because all the madness has ceased and desisted. I hate the idea that I resisted freedom for so long and consciously and subconsciously stayed to view and live through a storm called Michael. He didn't break my heart because it had already been broken over and over again…I just wanted him to be HIM."

"My Child,

I feel your heart and know that it is in the process of healing merely because of the fact that you are dealing with those emotions that had taken control and grabbed hold of your light. Continue to fight for understanding…understanding that some things may never make sense … that's no reason to straddle the fence and hold on through storm after storm that has proven to only harm you in the past. It didn't need to last forever if he never even made a true effort to see his own false reality as he pulled you in, again and again, causing pain after pain and strain after strain all at the cost of his personal gain and your emotional demise because he tried to drag you down not realizing that light can't be bound to dark…Without a switch. He is astounded now…dumbfounded now. You've taken back all the yesterdays, moved toward all the tomorrows and no longer had to hide the sorrow that he brought to your life. Now you make sacrifices that make sense…hence the proof that you gained. Never mind the pain…feel the joy as you destroy a fallacy…a myth that was presented as a gift that proved time and time to shift you off course. Force yourself to be strong and stay where you belong…in the light. My Child, you know what's right. Can't you feel that smile that is spreading in your being as you keep typing and freeing yourself and gathering what's left after the saga ended? Reach out to souls you've befriended for support. Abort this notion you've made into a dream that screams of confusion and distention. Don't mention it again. It was all make-pretend…play-play. Let him stay on the outside, weathering the tides if he chooses. Let him be the one who loses. What he eats can never make you shit unless you eat it. My Child, Love is and will always be. Know, understand, and accept the fact that I will never forsake thee."

I HEARD

I heard what you said,
saw what you did,
read your eyes, and
looked through you
and knew you were insincere
and yet… you think

I'm the fool.

SOMEONE TO LOVE

I'm used to having someone to love.
My heart aches from loneliness.
I'm not used to being lonely.
Empty flings without my heart can't satisfy me.
My heart's fate is linked to another. I'm not actually alone. I'm
not used to sleeping alone with no one to hold and help make me
feel secure. I'm not used to not saying his name and not seeing
his eyes. I'm not used to not sharing the secrets we shared. I'm
not used to not looking into his soul and not being a part of it.
I'm not used to not hearing him say my name and not feeling his
arms wrapped around me.
I'm not used to not feeling his love
and not giving him mine.
I'm used to having someone to love.

I WANT

I want to love you completely.
I want to be so into you
that you become me and I you.

I want to say your name

and feel my body respond...

by feeling all warm.

I want to feel you way deep down in my soul... so the

spirits take control...

and cause us to mesh, my flesh and your

flesh, deep into each other.

I want that bells ringing,

star seeing kind of love.

I want to trust you.

I want to confide in you.

But it's hard with all those ghost that linger quietly in the air,

occupying precious space

and time,

whispering in my ear...

showing me the way...

Trying to make sure that I don't get caught slipping,

reinforcing doubt, confirming suspicions,

causing the quiet to rule the day.

Have you ever put yourself in my shoes?

SEEING INTO THE FUTURE

Seeing into the future without facing the past is like looking at a movie without a cast. It's like running real fast without seeing the ground you have gained. It's like fire without the flame. It's like not remembering my name. It's like reading a book but not knowing what the book was called. Like being on a team without getting involved. Seeing into the future... without facing the past is just like a movie...without a cast.

HIS TOUCH

His touch is so sweet.
His eyes hold me captured.
His voice is the voice I long to hear.
Our conversation is deep.
Not too deep.
It's natural.
He makes me smile.
He makes me relax in him.
He is my friend.
Given time...
A love could grow between us until then,
I will continue to support this black man, continue to be his friend,
be his third eye, cause he only has two.
I'll watch his back when no one else is looking,

because I know he does the same for me. His touch is so
gentle…
and when he looks at me, I feel beautiful.

PLAY ANOTHER SMOOTH ONE

Play a smooth song on the radio for me. One that reminds me of
the way it used to be. One that soothes my mind… caresses my
soul…takes me back to days of old. One that takes me to a
different place… Where time can't be erased…what I
did…times we shared… When life was smooth… without a care.
Play a smooth song on the radio for me. One that reminds me of
the way it used to be.

MY THIRD EYE

Sometimes I don't see shit coming,
the reason for my third eye,
to catch what the other two miss,
to see the other perspective
from a different perspective,
to visualize the unseen, to penetrate, to see
through…everything…including…you.

THE BATTLE

What does the devil want with me causing me misery,

troubles that run so deep

there appears to be no bottom.

The tears sting my eyes so badly

I can't always see.

Ruptured heart hanging on by a vein,

a mind flooded with misinformation,

secrets and skeletons

that always pop up right before I see the light,

fewer days than nights,

robbing my joy,

stealing the faith,

diminishing the love,

tight as a glove,

taking my breath.

Will a tired heart be the cause of my death?

Glass ceilings and locked doors that in a better world would be

open to me.

False smiles,

fake affections,

Pain...the afflictions,

troubles...the infection.

Mouth wide open in silent and muffled screams, nightmares…

never dreams.

Nerves…jagged on edge,

 one foot on the ledge.

The fall is calling me,

whispering in my left ear,

covering my right,

distorting my 20/20 eyesight.

Panic set in a long time ago,

causing the illusion that I'm moving too slow.

Fast to others,

who could but would not know

that right now…

today

could just be my opening show.

My cries howl in the night,

lay dormant in the morn.

All day, waiting for the curtains to close,

giving me time to fold…

like the lawn chair…

at night…

that's me,

broke down like a baby…

Comforting myself…

Examining what's left of my life.

Time is flying. My spirit appears to be dying.

Am I tired of trying to maintain,

all the while, playing the devil's game,

with him toying with my mind,

and just like before,

putting dust where I shine,

causing my emotions to decline,

putting away my smiles,

trying to put out my light,

leaving me no delight.

But, am I tired of trying to maintain?

All the while playing the devil's game?

With a portion of my spirit left,

I'm all heart to the core

ready for this war.

I'll take him, pound for pound.

Ready to lay the devil's nagging ass down.

Enough was enough a long time ago.

He keeps trying me,

so I'll give him a show.

I'll lay him before me and

 with the knife he planted in my heart…

I'll cut that son of bitch apart.

Cut away the negative karma.

Set aflame his sins,

behind this predicament he has landed me in.

Cause right now, this minute...

It's on.

So devil, "Come with your fire,"

"tote your guns"

but, understand this,

if I swing, I'll be damned if I miss.

And this being the day you tote your guns,

this war you started

will be the war I won.

Your payback will be a mutha fucka.

You bitch ass, dick sucking, mutha fucka,

I'll pluck ya right of my shoulder,

mute that shit you whisper in my ear,

study your ass, study your fears,

put them in your face,

be that monkey on your back

that's itching to attack...

Cut no slack.

Hell, damn whispering in your ear,

trying to figure your satanic mind.

I'll have you lost where no one can find.

Fucking with me

got you caught up in some shit you know nothing about.

I don't talk shit that I ain't about.

Never saw me coming.

Thought you would leave me slumming.

Running? Flee…Who me?

Keep fucking with me and see.

See me from a distance,

know I'm about to speed up the pace.

In a minute….

I'll be all up in your face.

I'll be the last to see your eyes before your final demise.

The last to hear your bitch made cries.

You had better heed these words I'm saying,

cause trust me bitch, I ain't playing.

WHAT DOES THE DEVIL WANT WITH ME?

He wants my spirit,

the one that walks hand and hand with my soul.

He wants to break my mold, my identity,

the one that separates my soul from the others,

that could cause a cluster of confusion,

shatter the illusion…

Create reality,

show others what I see,

cause the shackles on our heads to break and set us free.

Free to evolve.

Free to explode with a serenity that few will ever know.

He wants the spirits that have the presence to take up an entire

room and make light the doom.

The spirits are reaching and touching the masses with a purity

that clashes with the devil's plan to destroy the Black man.

He needs my spirit...he wants to stop its flow because he knows

I won't keep his secrets.

His fate? Our positive spirits sealed it. I'm tired, damn near

outdone. The devil's got me too tired to run. So I'll stay and

stand and fight instead so my spirit will fly when my shell is

dead.

Chapter Five / Daddy is Just a Word

One thing was always in the back of my mind. I wanted to meet

my biological father. It finally came to pass in 2005. I was

around 35 or 36, living in Indianapolis, Indiana. Gail called and

said Daniel found our real dad, Danny Caurel, in Wake Forest,

North Carolina. Daniel and his "wife" Nora moved to Wake

Forest and lived with Danny, his wife, and their three children for a time. Yes, I had a sister and two brothers who were my children's ages living two hours away with the man mama replaced with Jackal. I had to see for myself. Gail gave me the contact information of one of our first cousins on our dad's side, Meka. Before I knew it, my kids and I were on the road on our way to Raleigh, North Carolina. This was my first time driving on a highway long distance. I'd never heard of GPS. The only directions I had were the directions on a MapQuest I'd written down. My nerves were torn all to pieces because anyone who knows me knows I prefer not to drive. I put that out of my mind because I was on my way to meet my cousin Meka, who would introduce me to my biological father.

The trip took 11 hours. That was 11 hours for me to imagine how my father would be. You could not tell me my daddy wasn't gonna be a great big, strong, blue-black, chocolate Mandingo type warrior man. I imagined him lifting a whole refrigerator all by himself. We arrived in Raleigh, NC, and were greeted with a rear tire blowing out on Capital Boulevard. A nice man and his son stopped and changed the tire. Then we were off on our way to meet cousin Meka. I liked her immediately and could not help but stop to think about what it could have been like to have cousins as friends. She took us to Auntie Lelia, who reminded me so much of myself that it was ridiculous. I was meeting cousin after cousin. It was overwhelming. I never thought about how meeting my father, and the rest of his family would make me feel. I remember being at one of Aunties functions, trying to pull myself together because it was all too much. Imagine meeting a whole family who knew exactly who you were.

Cousin Meka and one of her friends drove me to meet Danny. The ride from Raleigh to Wake Forest seemed to take forever and was very familiar in an unfamiliar way. It was as if I had ridden that ride a million times before in a past life. Danny lived way out in the country in a trailer in Wake Forest. I was in the backseat, trying to figure out how I was supposed to feel. I didn't know how to feel. I didn't know what to expect. I was about to meet my father for the first time. Danny's wife came to the door and seemed excited that I was there. I entered their home and stood in the living room as she made chit-chat that I could not hear. I was in a fog, realizing that my first encounter with my father was about to occur. About that time, a little ashy "teniny" frail man who was bald with curly hair on the sides with no teeth in the front emerged from behind a closed door. This was my father. I don't know what kind of reaction I expected him to have or what I expected his first words to be. He seemed emotionless as he looked at me and said (in a voice that sounded like Victor Newman from the soap opera "The Young and the Restless.") "What took you so long."

145

I knew then that Danny needed to have his coattail pulled so that he understood that I had a low tolerance for foolishness. It was clear that Danny had me confused with Daniel and Gail, who I am told broke down and cried in Danny's presence, and that's pretty much what I told him. I remember him being tickled at my "fire" and taking undeserved credit for it. The whole visit is like a blur of disappointment. I tried to like Dan. I really did. He had a way of ruining good moments by speaking....

"your father this," and "you're father that."

He went on and on, and all I could think was how unimpressed I was with his lack of regard for my presence like, "Where the hell have you been all my life?" Danny did a whole lot of posturing. Danny worked for the city of Raleigh. He drove a dump truck. He picked up trash on Aunties block. I was accustomed to seeing him on a specific day. One day stood out to me because I got excited when I saw the truck turning onto Auntie's block. I literally stopped in my tracks and had to catch my breath. I was excited to see my dad. A few days later, Danny asked me to dinner. He said, "I'm taking my daughter to dinner." I was ready when Danny arrived to pick me up. He was all dressed up. He had on wrinkled black dress pants and a white dress shirt, with the kind of white socks you wear with tennis shoes, and he had his teeth in, and it smelled like he sprayed a whole bottle of cologne on just for me. I smiled at his effort. We dined at

"Mayflower." I ordered an oyster platter. He said I was just like my mama and told me that oysters were her favorite when he knew her. Danny and I had the best conversation. He asked me a million questions about myself, and I asked him about himself. I told him I knew Danny couldn't take back all the missing yesterdays, but I was still willing to make a bunch of good tomorrows if he wanted to...and we agreed. Over dinner, he asked me to recite a poem for him, and I did. He seemed so proud of me. It was a perfect date. One Saturday morning, I heard a car pull into my driveway. Lo and behold, it was Dan dropping off some easels he just so happened to have found that he thought I might be able to use. Danny was growing on me. Things were going well until Aunt Dottie called me and called Danny on three-way. She told me to be quiet and just listen. I could not believe my ears. She brought up my name, and Danny went in. He started saying that Daniel, Gail, and I were jealous because he did not raise us. Danny called us clowns for no reason. He trash-talked my mama for at least 1/2 an hour. I sat quietly on the other end of the phone, taking in every hateful syllable from his mouth so I would never be fooled by him again. It's interesting how with so much to say, Danny never mentioned any of the stories his sister told me about him. Like how he abused mama, he never spoke about the two big dogs he forced my mama to walk. He never mentioned that even though mama was afraid of dogs, or how he hit her legs with a switch from a tree if she didn't walk fast enough. He never spoke about being so poor when we lived in New York that all mama cooked were potatoes and onions. All kinds of stories got back to me, like how Danny was strung out on drugs until the day he died. Oh, and how Danny's father supposedly threw a curse on him and how that was his excuse for being evil. His wife told me they found drugs on the property after he died. It was even suggested that he did not want to be in the hospital because he didn't want his blood tested. This so-called God-fearing self-proclaimed preacher was born full of hell and died full of hell. He left nothing behind except disappointment and bad memories. I saw him for who he was when my back was turned; that is who Danny was. When he died, I tried to be a respectful daughter. I attended his wake. It's crazy how nobody had anything nice to say about Danny when he was living, but in his wake, they did what people do…They lied and spoke highly of him. I will never forget it. At Dan's wake, a man stood and gave a flowery speech about what a good man Danny was, and he ended the speech by listing all of Danny's children. Some were names I never even heard of…some not even biological, and this little man had the nerve to end his speech and list with "and the other three," like me, Gail, and Daniel, didn't even have names. I raised my phone to my ear and pretended I was talking to someone as I quietly exited the building. I was done. I wished I never came back to North Carolina and never knew about or laid eyes on Danny. I never had a father. Neither one of them was worth a damn. My mama can sho pick them. That's all I have to say about my "long-lost daddy."

DADDY SAID

Daddy said that if they start it for me to finish it and that everything happens for a reason and for me not to live my life a lie. Daddy said I'm just like him. Daddy said I looked like I was born to speak and that he got a peep of the woman his little Robin had become. It did my heart good to see pride in my Daddy's eyes. I'm gonna love him because he is my father, and I see myself in him. He sits like I sit and watches as I do, and he shakes his head too the same way I do. Daddy said I am the hardest woman he has ever met, and I smiled on the inside because it's probably true and because he doesn't know what to do with me. Daddy said don't wait until it's too late and for me to remember that he has my back. He admitted that he could not take back yesterday, but today and tomorrow he plans to stay in my life because he wants to get to know me. When he crosses my mind, he finds me. It's better late than never…what if I had never met him? It would be a shame…Now I know his face and his name, and it's strange because it feels like I already know him. I think he could teach me to play chess real good and tell me all the things a Father should tell his daughter. He'll be pleased because I'll listen because I need to hear him in his wisdom that comes from him living and giving hell. The spell on him must have took cause it looks like he is finally trying real hard. I won't make it hard for him. I'll meet my father halfway. Yesterday is gone, and tomorrow

is looking good. Daddy said to see it as a blessing and make the most of it. I wanna like him… my Daddy…He reminds me of me. Daddy got all dressed up, put his teeth in, and put on cologne just for me. We sat over dinner and exchanged our minds to find common ground, and the familiarity of it all astounded me…I found in Daddy some of me. –to …Long lost Daddy, I Love You.

LONG LOST DADDY

Long dark winding roads leading to false forever have never fazed me. So, naturally, I arrived with understanding, not once demanding anything except closure, leisure more than deserved. He had the nerve to have excuses for the abuses he caused and used the law as a vice to make his lack of action right. Looking into my father's eyes, I tried to like. Still, I despised his nature and the creature that dwelled within him that controlled his flawed decision- making process

DANIEL

Maybe it was like he said. It doesn't change the fact that he left me for dead. The first thing he said was, "what took you so long?" and bragged about how strong I was.
After 35 years I tracked him down I found my father Who never bothered to know me.
The reality is…it is what it is. I truly dislike his ways. Thought after all this time I'd find closure instead my exposure to him has left me daunted.

Chapter Six / Fool me Once

There ought to be a law against loving someone that you put them before your own peace of mind. If keeping the "peace protects everyone except you, what sense does that make? Going home for a visit should not be a trigger. It should not leave you with bouts of depression. No one deserves to exist in a state of constant unrest behind things a child should never be expected to carry or swallow. My peace is more important than keeping the "peace."

It took me over forty years to lay the past to rest, and even then, it did not rest easy. In March of 2020, I returned to my childhood home to face demons and elephants that have always been in the room. The reality had always been what it was: My mother put a man before her child. Pure and simple. Prepared to go to war, if need be, I'd made up my mind to put everything on the line and say everything I needed to say while mama and Jackal were still on this earth. For as long as I can remember, my mother treated me like I was walking around with a pocket full of rocks, waiting for my moment to shatter the glass house she called "home." The day came when I went home on purpose to silence the noise in my head and clear air. Prepared for whatever, I'd speak my peace. I was going to ask Jackal what kind of man he must be to molest a child and how he could look at himself in the mirror, knowing his actions created a situation that allowed my mother to abandon her maternal instincts and turn her back on me. I would show no mercy, and I had no grace.

My friend Maria and I entered the house I was raised in and greeted Mama & Jackal. So, it couldn't be said that I caused a scene at mama's house, I asked Jackal to come outside on the deck with me while I smoked. He uncomfortably followed me to the deck. I lit a cigarette. He smelled of fear like he knew what was coming. As he visibly braced himself. I opened my mouth to announce that hell was at his door, and all that came out was,

"I forgive you. Neither of us is getting younger and would hate to leave this earth with words unsaid, so I forgive you."

He broke down and wiped snot with a cloth handkerchief he keeps in his pocket. I stood firm and as tall as trees. He opened his mouth to say something. I stopped him and said,

"Don't say anything. There is nothing you can say for yourself. Anything you say will change the course of this conversation. All I want to hear you say is what you're sorry for... What did you do to me?"

Jackal looked as if I'd asked him to cut his head off. It looked like it took everything in him to say through sobs,

"I.....MOLESTED... YOU."

Then I said,

"Now, doesn't that feel better? Take this as a gift, as weight you don't have to carry anymore. You can put it down. You can sleep easier now unless there are others."

He quickly interjected,

"No, Robin, it was just you,"

As if it was a good thing that he limited his perverted ways to just me.

That was the day after his 70th birthday. A calm came over me. I then understood why people say that forgiveness is more for the person doing the forgiveness than the person being forgiven.

***(A year later, I found out he was lying.) ***

Mama came out on the deck and noticed that Jackal had been crying. Instead of asking what was wrong, she just looked at him and shook her head, and said,

"He always crying about something."

I don't know why I only had my heart set on checking Jackal. At no time did I confront mama. We all went back inside the house. Jackal was so happy. In my mind, I honestly thought that it was over. I thought that now everything would be "normal." It wasn't, though. When I returned home to Durham, it occurred to me that they would think I was still lying unless Jackal told my siblings what he did. No one saw me forgive him or him admit what he did. It could have ended up being my word against his. I still looked like the daughter lying about "a good family man." I reopened the wound, called Jackal, and instructed him to tell my siblings the truth and that I was not lying. Jackal assured me that he would. A couple of days later, he called and said he had told Amiee what he had done to me. I asked him how the conversation went. He said just enough for me to know that he was lying. He finally admitted that he tried to tell Amiee what had happened but could not bring himself to tell her. I was irritated, but I let it go. I could understand why telling his daughter that he was a child predator would be hard to do. Almost a year passed before I returned to Chocowinity. This time I was coming home on business. It was November of 2020.

(I was 52, and Gail was 53.) Gail and I are both visual artists, and I'm a spoken word artist. I founded a movement called **"Breathe to Think**." In 2009 I created Breathe to Think to be a spotlight under which performing artist display. I created The Visual Arts Realm to do the same for visual artists. Wendy and our cousin Ray opened a shop in downtown Washington. Gail had access to the venue and was allowed to have an event there. She and I worked together and planned an art show to feature our art, and I would be the featured performer. Doing shows and performing was not new to me. I'd been doing art shows since 2009. Gail had never had an art show. We were tickled pink to have one together, and I was tickled pink to perform so close to my hometown. Chocowinity is across the bridge from Washington. Mama had never seen me perform before. I was so happy to be going home for a good reason and without the elephant in the room. Being a poet herself, I thought mama would appreciate a poetic setting.

I arrived at the Greyhound bus station with a suitcase that weighed 49 pounds and headed to my hometown of Chocowinity. I went home with the full expectation that now that everything was out in the open, I would not ever need to see my mother's ugly side again. No such luck would be mine. I intended to spend a couple of days with mama in Chocowinity and then go to Washington, NC and stay with Gail for the remainder of my visit. It made sense because Gail rented the sound system we would use and stored it in her apartment until the day of the show. Gail and I had a pre-show to-do list. It was not my plan to rehearse with mama present.

Mama asked, out of the blue, if I wanted to go see Gail. I agreed and didn't think anything of it. I put my suitcase away, and we went out the door to see Gail. We arrived, and everything seemed normal. The next thing I knew, mama asked if we were about to rehearse. I told her I had not planned on it, but I could go ahead and do the soundcheck since I was there. About that time, Gail asked me if I had finished a song I was working on. It just so happened that I had the track to the music she referred to on my computer. So, I naturally went into poet mode and performed the song for the mic check. Now mind you, this was not the first time my mother had heard my music. Suddenly, mama starting yelling,

"Don't sing that song. I'm NOT coming to your show if you sing that song!"

I guess mama took issue with a few cuss words in the song. By my way of thinking, mama was taking issue with something that had nothing to do with her. It was my event featuring my sister and me. I had been hosting and promoting this event for 12 years. As far as I have always been concerned, nobody can tell me how to run my business, not even my mother. So, I said,

"Well, Mama, in 12 years, you have never come to a Breathe to Think event. It is fine with me if you don't want to go to this one."

That should have squashed whatever issue mama was having. No such luck.

Mama started pacing back and forth, talking about how disrespectful I was. She accused me of saying I did not care what she thought. She was literally foaming at the sides of her mouth. Me being me, I decided to try and defuse the situation, so I said, "Mama, you are getting yourself all worked up. Calm down." I leaned in and hugged her with one arm because I had a cigarette in my other hand. Suddenly, mama yelled, "She's trying to choke me!"

You could have blown me over with a feather. It was a blatant, dangerous lie. I backed away from mama and braced myself for what would come next. I was unsure how Gail would respond to our mother saying I choked her. I didn't know if Gail would take mama's side and cause me to have to show my ass in her house. At that point, I was prepared for whatever. The saving grace was the fact that my Gail was standing there to witness everything that had just happened and said,

"No, Robin didn't. She just hugged you around the neck."

After lying on me to my face, all that mama had to say for herself was,

157

"Y'all can't take a joke."

At that moment, it was clear that mama reserved her ugly side for just me because Gail was clearly shocked. After all that, I knew I was not going back to mama's house to pretend she didn't just attempt to get me caught up in her lie. Instead, I spent the night at Gail's. The following day, I got a Greyhound ticket. I went back home to Durham, NC, to officially break down and cry over the unfairness and ugliness of it all. Even after going home and showing forgiveness, it was clear that mama was still the same mama who could throw evil fits for no reason. Moreover, she expected me to still act like nothing happened when she did.

A week went by, and it was time for the event. The host of Breathe to Think, OG, and I rode back to Washington for the show. Gail was there setting up the snacks for our guests when we arrived. She seemed genuinely excited, and I was too. Not long after, mama and Jackal arrived. They took a seat. I noticed that mama kept walking back and forth to the door as though she was looking for someone. I asked her who she was looking for. She said that her friend Vicky was supposed to be coming. I told mama not to worry about who came and who didn't because everyone who was meant to be there would be there. Mama smiled and finally relaxed and took a seat. When Amiee arrived a little while later, we embraced. I was tickled because she made her famous cupcakes for the event, and she seemed genuinely glad to see me. I was pleased to show my visual art along with my sister, and I was pleased to be able to share my poetry and song with my hometown. It was a very intimate setting. Before long, the show began. Gail and I took to the mic and discussed our creative process with the audience and explained the paintings we selected to show. There was a brief intermission before I performed a 45-minute set. The one thing that stood out to me the whole time I was performing was that every time I looked at mama from the stage area, she looked away from me. It troubled me. Jackal sat beside her, looking as wound up as a watch. After the show was over, OG drove me back home to Durham.

About a week later, Gail called and told me that Amiee told her that,

"Robin was not lying. He did it to me too."

I could hardly believe my ears. I don't think Gail realized the magnitude of this new information. It was almost like she felt through telling me that Amiee admitted that Jackal molested her when she was 14, I'd find some kind of closure. In this same conversation, Gail had a repressed memory emerge. Suddenly she claims to have remembered seeing Amiee's journal under her bed back in the day. Gail claims the book was lying wide open under Amiee's bed. She said she was not trying to read it…. but she read a little bit because it was open. In the journal, Gail claims that Amiee admitted to being touched by Jackal. Then all of a sudden, another repressed memory came back to her. For decades, I have always wondered what prompted mama to take me into Dan's room, slap me across the face, and tell me Jackal was her man. Now here Gail was confessing that she was the one who told Mama that Jackal was playing inappropriately with me. I was stunned. None of what she was saying made sense. Decades ago, I confided in Gail that Jackal was a child molester. Her exact response had been,

"He didn't do it to me, so why should I think he did it to you?"

I did not speak to Gail for years behind that statement. And now she was telling me that she told mama, which meant mama knew Amiee was molested by Jackal too. I gave Gail too much credit when I automatically assumed she would always have my back. Now the truth was finally coming to light. My family consisted of a bunch of liars and at least one pervert. They were all in on it, never mind the fact that their lies caused me to question my sanity. My mama had me halfway, believing that I imagined being molested by her husband. Come to find out, Jackal not only molested me, but he molested Aimee, his biological daughter too. Each time, rather than call the authorities and have the Jackal arrested, mama told both Amiee and me that we made it up. I saw red. Amiee waited her whole life to finally admit that

I was not lying. Here she was full grown with three almost-grown children, finally admitting that she was molested by Jackal, too. As far as I was concerned, all bets were off.

This is the same sister that Jackal claimed he tried to tell the truth to but could not bring himself to. When the reality was, there was no need for him to tell Amiee because she already knew he was a child molester. After all, he molested her too. I could see why Amiee did not speak up as a child, but at some point, during her adult life, she could have had my back and cleared my name. Instead, she went along with the rest of them and pretended that I was just "crazy Robin making my truth up." Then I thought, Mama and Jackal babysat Amiee's children while she worked. Why would Amiee allow Jackal and Mama to babysit her two daughters when they were little girls, knowing Jackal had a fetish for little girls? None of it made sense.

I asked Gail if Amiee had told her children about Jackal. Gail said that Amiee confided that she would not tell her children about it because they already had enough on their plates. It bothered me that Amiee was still trying to keep the secret even though her oldest daughter blocked me on Facebook and acted as if I stole from her. I could see if I had a relationship with this niece, but I have seen her on two...maybe three occasions. I have always gone out of my way to be kind to my oldest niece because I felt the awkward distance between us. I can only assume that in her mind, I am the evil auntie who lied about her granddad.

That day, I officially decided to finish writing this book. I'd had enough of the lies and dysfunction. I always knew I would write this book. Initially, I had planned on writing it after my mother passed away. It dawned on me that if I waited until my mother passed away, people could say I made it up. I need these words to fill the air so that all inquiring minds have a living source to go to if they have questions. I decided to throw caution to the wind and put it all on the line in this book. Initially, I planned to only write about my experience as a child. The more I wrote, the more it became clear that I had to tell my whole story. I needed to make the connection between the trauma that occurs and the decisions that people make based on trauma. I recognize that at some point, we all grow up and become adults and must take responsibility for our actions. I attribute many early decisions to the fact that my primary concern was to get away from Chocowinity, NC, and put it as far out of my mind as possible. In a sense, I was running from it. The thing about running is that you can be so busy running and looking back to ensure that whatever you are running from is not gaining ground that you run into all kinds of trouble. I ran into an abusive marriage, a relationship with a child predator, and a string of useless relationships that found me seeking anything resembling a family. Relationships that did nothing but break my spirit. After I stopped running and realized the pattern, I had to go about the task of finding myself and putting myself back together. A considerable part of my healing process was clearing my name. My family painted me as some crazy person who lied about Jackal. No one accused her of lying when Amiee's truth came to light. I knew I would do everything possible to ensure the truth was in the air. I never considered the consequences of writing a book about family secrets because it didn't matter to me. It didn't matter how my family responded or felt about it. All that mattered was that everyone was seen in their most accurate light. At this point in my life, I am getting too old to just leave things to settle. I am done being the bigger person. I am done just letting things slide. I am done putting other people's peace before my own. I am done. The reaction of others to my book is of no consequence to me. As far as I am concerned, if a person does not want the world to know their truth, they should make sure their truth is something they can face when walking in public. I wish I'd had the strength to finish this book years ago when my manager suggested it at the time. Grace said the first thing I needed to do was write my story to establish myself as a public speaker and a subject matter expert to do some good. I delved in and got to writing. The bulk of this book was written years before I went to Chocowinity on July 4, 2021, to confront Mama and Jackal. I stopped writing it because I have a heart. I could not imagine how mama would feel after it was published....so I stopped. I wanted to spare Mamma's feelings even though she never considered mine. I knew the book would break her, and I didn't want to feel how it would feel knowing my mother was feeling some type of way behind something I did. At the end of the day I put my feelings first

Chapter Seven / When Siblings Attack

The closer I came to completing this book, the more I saw people's true colors. Gail was the only family member who still spoke to me after I started promoting the book. I first noticed her disconnect in April of 2021.

Gail and I share the same birthday; I was born exactly a year after her. This year, for some reason, I knew I would not hear from her on our birthday. Sure enough, I didn't. The last time I'd spoken with her, she said she was planning to come to visit me on our birthday and would call me later that evening to let me know, one way or the other. My phone rang 15 days later. None of me could be convinced that Gail was not in cahoots with mama and her silent treatment.

Out of the blue, I received a Facebook message from Gail. In it, she said that she was uncomfortable having conversations with me because her words showed up in this book's promotion. She went on to say that she would be glad when the book was published and for sale. She said that she had no intention of reading it. She said that on a personal level, she was sick of it. She claimed she was getting calls and messages from people who didn't give a damn about her, me, or the family. She said she loves her family so much, but she hates where we are now. She said she thinks about us, and she is brought to tears. She went on to say that three people had to meet her wrath in the past week after questioning her about my book. She claimed that they came at her out of vindictive nosiness. Then she wrote that she had her trauma too, but she never put me in a position where I had to deal with her trauma. She went on to say that she "walked that shit alone".... Then she said that everything is about perspective and everybody's perspective is different.

I just shook my head at her attempt to throw the scent off of the fact that she was the dog carrying bones. Gail and I discussed writing my book. She knew what I was writing and even permitted me to write my book.... her and mama both. Gail went so far as to have countless conversations with me for hours. I'd tell Gail my memories, and she confirmed each and every one with the understanding that I was writing my book. I can't count how many times I said,

"Say that again. I want to make sure I get it right in my book."
Mama and Gail both gave me their permission to write my book.
It is clear that they never dreamed I would write it. It seems it
was alright for me to write the book unless I actually "wrote" the
book. I can only deduce that Gail is scrambling to find a way to
make it appear that I tricked her into divulging all the family
secrets. How is Gail going to convince anyone that she was not
the dog carrying the bones? Common sense would tell me not to
disclose personal information to someone writing a book about
it. That would be the last thing I would do if I didn't want the
information made public. How would I know that the morning
after Gail found Amiee's journal and gave it to mama, Amiee no
longer had rules she had to obey? The way I understand it, it's
like her silence was bought. I know that Dan was supposedly
cleaning a gun when it just happened to go off and shoot straight
to the wall right above Jackal's side of the bed. I know that
Jackal was molested by one of his sisters because Gail told me. I
didn't write about that because child molesters are quick to say
they are child predators because they were violated as children.
That dog does not hunt in my world. Being violated as a child is
no excuse to turn around and molest children when you grow up.
How would I know that Jackal has a kid no one talks about?
How would I know that mama pulled a knife on her sister
recently? Amiee never told me she was molested. She never

166

apologized for keeping quiet while my name was slandered. Throughout it all, Amiee never did one single solitary thing to make me feel like she was my sister. It is the ultimate betrayal. I understand her being silent when she lived under mama's roof. At some point, Amiee grew up, and the side she chose was against me and had no problem letting me question my memories. But now, in a Facebook message, Gail is acting like a wounded sister that was tricked into revealing family secrets. It's interesting how once Amiee came out about being molested, suddenly, Gail started having one repressed memory come up after the other. I didn't believe her then, and I don't believe her now. I am a lot of things, but I am not a fool. Gail knew the entire time and pretended she didn't. As far as I am concerned...when I confided in her all those years ago, she betrayed me. She can act mad all she wants to, but the reality is I am the one who should feel some kind of way....not her. She picked her side.

In a string of messages on Facebook and text messages, Gail said,

"You're full of shit. You fucked up. Go make your millions. You are dead to me. You are the most vindictive person I know. It's sad that you are this way. You are completely dysfunctional. You are indeed writing your own story, and the ending remains to be seen. I mourn our sisterhood, and that's it.....Goodbye, Sneaky Robin."

To which I replied,

"Ya Mammy."

I meant it. Is clearing my name and standing up for myself vindictive? If it is, then call me vindictive. Is it really sad that I am the way I am? I love myself and adore that I have heart and will go toe to toe if need be. I don't need to be told that I am writing the book I said I would write. My ending is not written, but I can say this...my ending will be on my terms. My ending will not involve me putting the feeling of folks who never had my back before my own. If I make millions by selling this story, it's the least I deserve. I make no apologies or offer excuses for my actions since I learned they all knew and still painted me in the corner as a crazy Robin.

Less than a week later, I received a message in my Facebook inbox out of the blue. It was a screenshot of a Facebook post Daniel made. It read (as if someone asked his opinion)

"Here is my take on the so-called tell-all book. Not trying to justify anyone's actions...but the storyline is exaggerated and fabricated fluff (for attention and shock value). I know because I was there....and SHE was off the chain. She needs to keep it 100 and just say she is doing bad and simply trying get to a bag (money). She's gonna have to lie and exaggerate to make it a

good read....... I get that I. really do. But the moment she attempts to market it as truth over fiction, she'll be legally liable, But the real question that's pressing is what kind of person attempts to destroy her own 70- plus-year-old mother (who has only shown you love your whole life.... for... for a bag? Get some treatment, take your meds, and leave our mother's name out of your twisted mouth."

As I read his words, I knew I would make him pay for every syllable, space, and punctuation in his blatantly disrespectful post. All bets were off where he was concerned because his post was victim-shaming at its all-time best. If showing love is lying to your daughters and telling them they imagined being molested, I don't want that kind of love. There is no exaggeration in this book. Where is the lie? Daniel is the same person who lied and told his ex-wife that our mother was a prostitute on the streets of New York, and we all ate out of trash cans. We were not raised in New York. Daniel and I were born in New York.... We've never lived in NY growing up...as infants, toddlers, or young children. Daniel lied and said he was Jamaican...had people asking me why I didn't have an accent. I've never even been to Jamaica. Daniel even had "Dan Dred" on his license plate and everything. Daniel is the last person who should accuse anyone of lying and exaggeration. Daniel is known to lie like a rug...and he had the nerve to accuse me of exaggerating.

Nowhere in Daniel's post was there even the slightest mention of Jackal outside of,

"Not trying to justify anyone's actions…But the storyline is exaggerated and fabricated fluff."

The word "but" negates everything he said. There is no mention that a child molester is being harbored and protected at my mother's house to this day. I damn near had a nervous breakdown behind this and was in therapy and on meds for years, thinking I made it up because mama said I did. I suffer from PTSD, anxiety, and depression— behind my family being the enemy. I'm back in therapy, and I take meds every day. Writing this book set me back mentally because I had to revisit all the memories I had stored away. How can Daniel be so flippant about mental health when he needs a therapist right now himself? Daniel is protecting a sexual predator and his enabler. Daniel has not read my book, has no idea what the storyline is, and has not spoken to me in years. Suppose he was "there," as he claims in his post. In that case, he should have had a brave heart and protected his sisters instead of posting his yearly Father's Day posts about how a child predator taught him to be a good man.

Chapter Eight / The Confrontation

I confided in Grace about how my siblings' reactions bothered me. I didn't understand how they could still act like I was the villain in the story. She let me vent and then casually asked, "Wouldn't it be nice if you could get some proof?"

If I'm to keep it 100%, my brother Daniel is the real "hero" for going online, accusing me of exaggerating. His accusation is why I knew I had to go home one last time and lay this matter to rest.

The goal was to go home and speak my peace. Maria drove me there just like she had driven me two years before to show Jackal forgiveness. My heart beat faster and faster the closer we came to Chocowinity. It was an impromptu trip, like when I came home to face the child molester two years prior. This time, I was confronting both the molester and my mother, the enabler.

I arrived at 1:55 PM on the 4th of July 2021. The ride there was an emotional roller coaster. I was popping up out of the blue to demand answers from my mother, who had not spoken to me in over 8 months because of a book she gave me permission to write. I'd planned on giving Jackal a full clip of verbal punishment for lying to me two years ago when I initially forgave him. He'd told me he'd never molested anyone other than me, so it was easy for me to forgive him based on his lie. When I asked him to tell my siblings that he was a child molester, he told me he tried but could not bring himself to do it. A year later, Gail called and informed me that Amiee confided in her that Jackal molested her too and that "Robin was not lying."

The closer we came to arrive, the more anxious I became. It is true what the old folks say, "everything good for you does not feel good." Pulling into the driveway, I noticed all the cars were there. Mama and Jackal were home. I opened the car door and walked to the side door of the house as confidently as I could. The little girl in me was terrified of upsetting my mother. I knocked for over 5 minutes. Finally, looking through the glass window on the door, I saw my mother emerge from the end of the hallway. She was carrying an oversized book. I'd later discover that it was a bible she clutched to herself. Mama approached the door. Instead of opening it, she lifted the bottom piece of glass on the storm door and spoke to me through it, "Hey, Robin,"

Mama said awkwardly.

I found it odd that she didn't open the door and seemed so calm because she had not spoken, emailed, or returned a text to me in over 8 months. My birthday came and went with no words. Mother's Day came and went with no words, and here she was, acting like sweetness and light in the softest voice, peeping through the button of a screen door at me as if I was going to harm her.

"Hey, Mama,"

I replied.

Mama was peering down the driveway at the car I'd gotten Out of.

"Who you got wit chu?"

she asked.

"Maria is in the car, but I am by myself,"

I replied.

"Is anything wrong.... are you here to..."

Mama said before I interjected,

"I'm coming here to be peaceful."

"Are you sure?"

Mama asked.

A part of me was a little irritated. I have never disrespected my mother or her home. I assured her that I came in peace. Once satisfied, mama stepped away from the door and said,

"Let me come outside."

In all the years I have visited my mother, she has never refused to let me into her home. I felt like a stranger. She cracked the door just wide enough to step onto the deck. Again, I was a little irritated because, in my mind, mama had a lot of nerve acting like I was not welcome in her home. While a child predator was welcomed and lived inside that same house. Rather than start off on the wrong foot, I let it go and spoke clearly,

"I really wanted to ask Jackal something too."

Seeing mama stiffen up, I went on to say,

"Mama, I don't like any of this. I just wanted to see if we could clear the air."

To which mama replied,

"Did you come here for peace, or did you come here to start something?"

Mama spoke as if it were my nature to come to her home with drama. The reality was that I had never brought drama to her door. In fact, the previous year, when I came home and forgave Jackal for being a child molester, I took him outside to avoid drama. It amazes me how people can paint others out to be what they aren't to avoid dealing with the reality of their own nature.

"I came here for clarity, I replied.

My answer seemed to satisfy mama, who motioned me to sit in a lawn chair. Out of nervous energy, I opted to stand instead. It struck me as odd that Jackal did not come outside with mama. He'd been standing in the doorway, and now, he was nowhere to be seen. I knew there was no way I was letting him off the hook, so I asked mama to ask Jackal to join us on the deck. She called out to him and stood waiting. After a few minutes Jackal awkwardly made his way from inside the house onto the deck. I could see no reason to drag the conversation out, so I got straight to the point,

"Hello, Jackal…All I wanted to say to you was…."

Before I knew it, I was overwhelmed with emotion and sobbing like a child. It was as if the weight of the world was on my shoulders. Mama kept saying,

"Keep it together."

As if that was even possible. I was hanging on by a thread, and I knew it. Amid attempting to have the most difficult conversation I had ever had, I kept reminding myself to breathe. Mama suggested that I take a seat. This time I obliged because I could feel my knees shaking under me. I gathered my composure and began again. I reminded Jackal of the

last time we stood on the deck. I reminded him of my act of forgiveness. Before I could say more, mama interjected,

"Do you have something in your pocket recording me?"

I could not believe my ears. Mama sounded just like a guilty person to me.

"Why would you care if you are in the right?" I countered.

"Let her finish what she has to say," Jackal interjected.

"Go ahead," mama said.

Looking directly at Jackal, I said through tears,

"I did not want to pop up on y'all, but this is what it is now. The last time we stood here, I told you I forgave you. I meant it, and you know I meant it with all my spirit."

"I know,"

Jackal said.

I went on to add,

"And a year later, when Gail called and told me that Amiee said you did it to her, too..... I knew then that you were a liar....It made me think back to when I forgave you...when I told you to tell Amiee that you were a child molester. You said you tried to, but you couldn't bring yourself to tell her. It made sense to me at the time, or at least I wanted it to. After all, Amiee is your biological daughter. "

Nowhere in my wildest imagination would I have ever thought that Jackal would molest his own blood daughter. I felt guilty for leaving Amiee there with a child predator. A part of me took responsibility. If I could have had the courage I have now, my baby sister would not have suffered at the hands of her father. I wondered how my mother lived with herself, knowing she knew about both Amiee and me.

I went on to tell Jackal,

"I believed you when you said you could not bring yourself to tell her, and I just let it go because I felt like I could understand why you could not tell your daughter that you were a child predator. When in reality, she already knew because you molested her, too. So, from where I am standing...everybody knew, and everybody pretended."

I wondered how they all thought I would respond once I realized that it was indeed a family secret that the whole family kept. I don't think I was supposed to know about Amiee's molestation. If I knew that they were aware of Amiee being molested by Jackal, logic would follow that I would know they made me believe I was crazy.

Mama took it upon herself to claim she once again did not know and imply that I was there to argue. I assured her that I was only there to clear the air. She insisted that I was arguing and. I insisted that I was not. And looked towards Jackal and asked him,

"I want to know if you can see where I am coming from."

No matter how much of a good man he pretended to be, it did not negate the fact that he had a fetish for doing things to little children that a "good man" would never do. Jackal had to know that I would return when I found out he had lied. I think he crossed his fingers that he would get away with it. When I forgave him the first time, I honestly meant it. I was going to let it all go and move on. After all, you can't forgive someone while harping over what you claim you forgave them for. By my way of thinking, I had no choice but to bring hell to his door, but I arrived peacefully. Instead of the family turning on me the way they did, I think they should all be kissing my ass because it took me this long to get strong enough to call them all out.

Jackal stood like a crooked preacher prepared to give a sermon he'd rehearsed over and over again when he began speaking,

"Robin, I am only about one thing, and that's forgiving and forgiveness."

He was confident and had a lot of nerves speaking to me as if he thought he could justify molesting his wife's daughters. There he was talking about forgiveness as though he deserved it. He had a lot of nerves, considering the last time I forgave him was based on his bald-faced lie.

Not even slightly impressed, I responded,

"You would be about forgiveness because you need forgiveness."

Jackal kept right on talking,

"Robin, I can't undo what I have done. I can't make history all over again. I done wrong, and I'm sorry, and that's all I can do. If you forgive me...you forgive me. If Amiee forgives me…she forgives me. If Gail forgives me…she forgives me, and if your mama forgives me…. she forgives me."

Without even a pause, he went on to say,

"Because if I live in the past, I will be a dead man tomorrow. If you live in the past, you gone be a dead man tomorrow. Like I say, we gon just have to let it go and ask the Lord to forgive us. I spent a lifetime trying not to repeat my sins. I just can't keep living in the past. It can only destroy me, your Mana, and everybody. Amiee and all of them, they decided to move on and just let it go cause they know you can't change the past. We all made mistakes. We all have done terrible…terrible things…me, you…all of us done terrible things in our lives."

Jackal must have spent years coming up with his speech. From his soapbox, he preached. I disagreed and wondered who the "we" and "all of them" Jackal made mentioned were. I had to stop him there. There was no way he was about to include me in their madness. I interjected,

"I ain't did no terrible things."

His mask cracked a second before he said,

"Thank God you haven't, but it's a lot of us…."

Jackal was one step from saying,

"I'm not the only one who has molested children,"

as if numbers made it make sense. He said all of that as if, in doing so, he had made everything right. Jackal showed little to no regard for the damage done to my life. He took no responsibility for the breakdown of the relationship between my mother and me. Jackal said it all as if to say there was nothing I could do about it, so I might as well forgive him and move on. He said it as if forgiveness was a guarantee. Mama sat there looking proud, like she was listening to a preacher preaching or an entirely different conversation.

He switched up and said,

"I'm not the only one that's done it…I have done terrible things, and I am thankful the Lord forgave me, and I was able to forgive myself and the people I done it to. I haven't been a saint. I'm sorry, and I'm hoping you can get past all this."

I don't know which was more unsettling...Jackal not mentioning the lie about never molesting anyone else or mama acting like Jackal's excuse of an apology was admirable. Either way, I was done with both of them. I knew there was no coming back from any of it. I had to do what it took to lay their baggage down at their door. It was the lack of remorse for me. Jackal took on a "get over it" air. The other thing that stood out to me is that he included Gail in the list of people who needed to forgive him. It would not have stood out if Jackal had mentioned everyone who lived in the house, but Jackal didn't. A part of me wondered if he included Gail because she was a victim too. If that was the case, that would mean all those years ago, Gail lied when she said, "It didn't happen to me, so why would I believe it happened to you?"

I have always reflected on her words. I was crushed by them. The more I thought about it, the less sense the emergence of Gail's "repressed memories" made. It was too much of a coincidence that repressed memories that pointed to Gail being aware that Jackal was a child predator all along came up after Amiee confessed. It was all too much. As I sat there looking at this feeble-bodied man trying to act like there was a way to justify his action, I knew one thing. I knew I would not carry the baggage that belonged to my mother and her husband one more day. I would leave it all right there where it began.

Just imagine being me at that moment. I was overcome with sadness that stayed with me. Mama was sitting there looking up at Jackal with such admiration. I should have screamed,

"What about me mama? What about your child?!"

Mama chimed in and said,

"You don't know what it took for Jackal to tell me everything that happened."

The question is, when exactly did Jackal tell mama that he was a child predator? Was it before he was forced to admit it or decades ago? Either way, Jackal gets no cool points for confessing that he is a child molester. Yet here mama sat, acting proud of him. You could have blown me over with a feather. My mother still defends the man who molested Amiee and me. Mama acts like he should be rewarded for telling the truth that I forced him to tell...the truth she already knew. I literally cried through the entire conversation.

As my mind was blown by her logic, I replied,

"I don't care how much you claim it took him to tell you. He is a child predator that lives in this house with you."

To which she responded,

"That's what you said."

No, that is what Jackal said right in front of her during the exact conversation. Yet here she sat defending the child predator.

Mama went from saying, "I made it up," to "I dreamed it," to "I made it up because I was spoiled and could not have my way." With the truth staring her dead in the eyes, she acted as though her husband had not just admitted to being a child predator. Finally, I said,

"I'm just calling it what it is."

That's when mama interrupted me and said,

"Let me ask you a question...and you stand right here before this Bible..."

Before she could go into her dramatics, I politely told her that the book meant more to her than it did to me. I couldn't believe that mama was standing there clutching a bible and protecting a child predator simultaneously. I didn't understand how mama could have the nerve to stand and act holier than thou, knowing she's never taken me to church a day of my life. It's funny how when people get old, they find religion. It's like Mama and Jackal took turns saying the Lord forgave them. The Lord may have forgiven them, but I have a long memory.

I was one step from saying,

"If the bible means so much to you, mama, how do you think God feels about you putting that man before your children?"

Before I could fix my mouth to say the words, Jackal jumped in and reminded mama of her anxiety. Jackal had a way of looking like he was defusing volatile situations. When it was clear that Jackal was really stopping conversations before, they went so far and the truth came out. Every time I came close to checking my mother, Jackal always jumped in and acted like he was defending me.

"I will not let you talk to your daughter like that!"

He would say.

His words always snapped mama back to the reality that she had more to lose than me. My heart was broken into a million pieces because mama had the perfect opportunity to apologize, and she never took it. My biggest fear my whole life was that my mother would leave this earth without making it right. I stood before my mother, looked her in the eyes, and told her that she was my greatest disappointment but that I forgave them. I told her I would no longer pretend with them and that if things could be any other way than what they were, they would be.

Jackal fixed his mouth to say,

"I know it's different than it should be. Maybe in time, it will be different."

I overlooked him and told my mother,

"I came here because, who knows, we are both getting old, and you're not speaking to me. I didn't want to get a call one day letting me know that my mother has left this world without us having our final discussion."

To which mama replied,

"Well, I hope this ain't our final discussion. You know, I think about you every day of the year. I admit I used to see you on Facebook. I had to stop seeing it because it was going on and on and on, and it was giving me anxiety and stressing me out. I felt like I was getting sick, so I had to get away. I think about you all the time, and I pray that one day… It's the strangest thing. I know y'all young people got something against the Bible…but it's the strangest thing that I read this here Bible today….and you popped up.

To which I replied,

"Don't you always read it, Mama?"

My question went unanswered as she went on to say,

"I pray for you. I pray for all my children. I pray for you all the time that you would have peace of mind one day… and that I have peace of mind and everybody else in the family have peace of mind and one day we can be halfway decent to each other."

I was glad she brought up "all her children" because it reminded me to tell her,

"When you talk to Daniel, tell him he has crossed me the worst way. That's all I want you to say to him.

Mama's response was,

"I can't tell Daniel that."

Even so, I knew she would… so I went on to say,

184

"My siblings are coming at me like they want war. If they want war, they can get it. Tell them to leave me alone, mama."

To which mama replied,

"Don't nobody want no war. Ain't nobody gonna bother you."

Her response was almost laughable. She thought I was afraid of them when the reality is...I was scared for them. My mother has me completely baffled. I believe she loves me. I just don't understand how she could. In my world, there are some things you just don't do. I looked at mama and wondered where the disconnect was because there was no way in the world she and I could have been listening to the same conversation. The blank look in her eyes made me wonder if there was anything inside. No matter how hard I try, I don't understand what kind of mother could sit there and watch her daughter genuinely weep and not respond. What kind of mother could sit and listen to her husband all but admit to molesting all of her daughters and show no emotion? She did not look the least bit bothered. Her only concern was that people were reading about it on "Facebook." I hate the day my sister ever gave Mama her Facebook login. It bothers me that mama is lurking in the background and caring more about what strangers on Facebook think about her than what her daughter thinks. I wondered what type of mental defect would make a mother paint her daughter out to be the bad guy and the predator out to be the one she needs to defend. Mama went on to say,

"You know, I had told Gail to tell you that I love you the next time she talked to you,"

As she gazed at me for approval, I quietly said,

"It didn't feel like it...You stopped talking to me."

"I did, but I can tell you why I stopped talking to you,"

Mama replied.

I interjected,

"But you didn't stop talking to Jackal." she countered,

"Well, Jackal ain't never talked to me like I was this tall."

She pressed her thumb and pointer finger together to demonstrate the word small. My mind was blown. What in the world did she mean by saying this man never made her feel small? This man molested at least two of her daughters. To hear her tell it, "He never made her feel small. Yet somehow, I made her feel small by telling her the truth. It was the saddest, most ignorant thing I have ever heard come out of my mother's mouth. Instead of pointing out the obvious that she either overlooked or could not see, I simply responded,

"Well, I spoke to you how I felt was according, and I meant everything I ever said, wrote, or recorded."

Looking me in the eyes, mama said,

"That video you sent me...the way you was talking to me... I knew you had to hate me with a passion to send me

186

something like that. In my mind, I thought we were getting along good, and then it was like you popped up on Facebook, and I was shocked."

"Do You know why?"

I asked and went on to say, "

"It was exactly what you said it was. We were getting along so good. I was coming down home to visit every chance I got. I loved every minute of it. I never hated you, not one day in my life. Anybody who knows me knows that I adore my mama, and I give you a whole lot of credit for a lot of stuff I am good at. I don't have any reason to set myself up to be on the outside looking in like I've always been when I'm finally getting along and everything is good. I came home and forgave Jackal. A year passed. Then Gail called me and told me that Amiee told her that it happened to her too and that I wasn't lying.... That's when the whole bottom fell out. Because it just dawned on me that I believe it happened to Gail too. …. Jackal doesn't have to own up to it. But I can't imagine Jackal skipping a child.

Mama was quick to come to Jackal's defense when she said, "No, that's where you are wrong at."

The truth was mama could pretend all day that she did not know Jackal was a child predator when it was just me accusing him of being one, but when Amiee came out, mama was pinned to the wall. Now she had two daughters saying the exact same thing about her husband. She had two daughters saying that their mother told them they made up molestation accusations through dreams and writing stories.

To which I responded,

"But you don't know, mama. I don't believe Gail. Because Gail has "repressed memories" popping up all the time."

Mama went on to say,

"They all say you have repressed memories," she replied.

I wondered who the "they all" she mentioned were. My story has never changed. It is maddening to be accused of lying by liars. Before I could correct her, Jackal finally found his tongue and chimed in,

"Robin, you said you did not come here to rehash this."

No, what I said was that I came to clear the air. I don't see how Mama and Jackal expected the air to be cleared without rehashing their lies. I reminded Jackal that it was mama who brought up the topic.

It was the hardest, longest conversation I ever had with my mother, and nothing changed at the end of the day. Her biggest concern was the fact that I was promoting the book on Facebook. She didn't care how I felt. She did not care that her children were estranged. She let Jackal control the conversation and never once answered to her part in any of it. She allowed this little feeble-bodied man to speak to me as if he could dismiss me from the conversation that I started.

My own mother did not invite me into the house I was raised in. As I made my way to depart, she insisted that I literally step a foot in her home so that I could not go back and say she did not invite me in.

It was odd because the house felt unnaturally clean. It dawned on me that mama overcompensated for the fact that her home was anything but "clean" by making it appear immaculate. There were so many more questions that I could have asked my mother. I guess it just goes to show that the child in us remains. It's easy to call out the child predator. It's almost impossible for me to call out my own mother. Plus, I know her. I knew that she would shut down completely if I came down hard on her. Mama will never admit to knowing that Jackal is a child predator. I remember that day she said,

"I don't know how all this could have happened without me knowing. Sometimes I look at Jackal and think I will shoot him in the head."

I wanted to say,

"What good will that do now, Mama?"

I don't know who she thinks she is fooling. Mama knows that Jackal knows, mama knows that Gail knows, mama knows that Amiee knows, Daniel knows, and mama knows that I know. The crazy thing is, I am the only one who acts like I know. Until a year ago, that whole family still celebrated birthdays and holidays like there was no elephant in the room. I was finally confronting the source of my sorrow. There were so many questions I did not ask mama and so many things I wanted to say:

- I wanted to tell mama that I never broke her heart. I just broke the silence.
- I wanted to tell mama that she had no right to be angry at me for writing a book that tells the truth.
- I wanted to tell my mama that only a sick, twisted person would attempt to convince her children that they were lying when they were telling the truth.
- I wanted to tell mama that the games she plays with her children cost them each other.
- I wanted to tell my mama that there was never a secret because I told anyone who would listen.
- I wanted to tell my mama that she doesn't get to be mad at me for pointing out that she carries equal if not more blame than that little man she chooses to protect.
- I should have reminded my mama that she caused
- me to need therapy because she made me question my memories.
- I wanted to tell my mama that she is not angry...she

is embarrassed because now the world can see her nature.

- I wanted to tell mama that she does not get to be mad because this was all her doing when she decided to side with the child molester.
- I wanted to tell mama that she does not get to dictate how I heal.
- I wanted to tell my mama she should be ashamed of herself.
- I wanted to tell my mama that she does her children no good pitting them against one another.
- I wanted to ask my mama if it was worth it.
- I wanted to tell my mama that she does not get to act like she is clueless when the evidence proves otherwise.
- I wanted to tell my mama I spent my whole life trying not to be like her.

The list of unanswered questions will go unanswered. That's the most infuriating part of this whole story. It became abundantly clear that no amount of reasoning would cause my mother's maternal instincts to kick in. She is lost to me. The more we spoke, the more the conversation went left. In the end, Jackal reminded mama of her anxiety. And just like that, I was dismissed.

"Well, Robin, we appreciate you coming."

I went home and became dangerously close to the point of mentally snapping

Carter's final Chapter (inserted during publication)

Carter's chapter in my life ended on August 31, 2022, the day of our son Pauly's wedding. It was a bright and cheery wedding day. I'd gone back and forth about going to the wedding. I questioned whether going would be a trigger for me since Carter would be there. I had a series of depressive and anxiety episodes in the weeks leading to the marriage. I didn't know how to feel about sharing a joyous occasion with Carter and his wife. I didn't know how it would make me feel to see the man I once loved...the man who physically abused me with a wife who never saw that side of him. I knew it would hurt. I vowed to not go because I had to consider my mental well-being. No part of me wanted to be a stain on his otherwise perfect wedding day for Pauly. I wanted to see my Big Baby in his tuxedo marrying his Bride. I wanted to experience being the mother of the groom. I wanted to stand in my purpose and be the Matriarch. Pauly is the first of my children to be married. His happiness was contagious.

In the end, I put my feelings aside because all that mattered was that Pauly was happy. Ally drove from Wilson, NC, to Raleigh to attend her brother's wedding. She swung by, picked me up, and off we went to the wedding.... running a tad bit late. We arrived minutes before the wedding began. As I walked toward the wedding party standing outside, the first person I saw was Carter. I'd expected to see him and nod a silent hello. I didn't expect him to be the first person to greet me. It was too much. I avoided the greeting and stood with Malcolm, who walked me to my seat once the wedding started. Pauly was so happy and so proud. It was all over him. It was a beautiful ceremony. When it was done, we were introduced to "Mr. and Mrs. Carter in a room filled with love.

I made my way back outside and sat in the sun on purpose. I knew Carter wouldn't want to be in the sun. I was mistaken because here he came coming. Carter greeted me as I sat and peered up at him trying to get a glimpse of who Carter was before he went bad in my mind. Carter seemed nervous. There were plenty of people he could be talking to. I was trying to understand why Carter was right next to me every time I turned around, attempting to have minor chit-chat. I went on and mixed and mingled with my family. After dinner, I went to the deck area for a quiet moment to gather myself. People never believe me when I say I'm shy and don't like being around a lot of people. Just as I'd collected myself, Carter approached. He hugged me as if he was about to leave. Then he looked at me and said,

"I know you don't think people change. I changed. I'm not that evil person anymore. "

I had no words. Never in my wildest imagination did I ever think Carter would have this conversation with me. He went on to say,

"I have had therapy with myself."

I asked,

What did the Dr. say? Was there a diagnosis?

He said,

"No, I mean I am having therapy with myself. Believe it or not, I never put my hands on a woman after you."

I felt tiny pricks behind my eyes. I willed myself not to cry and said,

"Why was it me?"

Carter was speechless. I felt him feel my pain for the first time. My eyes were one step from exploding pricks of pain when I asked,

"What did I do?"

Carter shook his head and said,

"Robin, you were just being you. I'm not that evil person anymore."

"You know I wrote a book, right?

I asked, watching him react. He brought his hand to his head and made a motion that didn't look pleased.

I went on to say,

"And you have your own chapter."

He hugged me. Then he stopped hugging me. Then he looked at me and hugged me again. I turned away from him. I didn't want him to see me cry. I faded to the background in the corner of a joyous event and silently broke down. Not a soul knew. I felt every bit of hurt from way back when right then. I felt the pain from old tears trickle through my eyes. No matter how hard I tried to stop them, they fell. I heard the thump of them all, and all I could do was keep sticking out my chest like a child trying not to cry. I turned to face him. He was gone. In his place stood smiling up at me were Cahir, Leo, Kaz, and Tessa, my grandbabies. They were right on time. I snapped out of it and carried on.

After the wedding ended, when Ally and I left the car, I told Ally what had taken place between her father and me. I told her how much lighter I felt. Ally was happy to hear that there was finally peace there.

I am triumphant. I didn't need to confront Cater like I did mama and Jackal because Carter brought it to me on everything but bended knees. Maybe Carter used the wedding to own up to being the meanspirited man I always said he was. His wife had to be in the background encouraging him because otherwise, where was she while he was mustering up the courage? I realize that Carter cannot change the past or give back what he took from my life, but he finally stopped saying,

"Forget about the past. Stop bringing up the past."

I felt redeemed.

The very next day, imagine my shock when Ally told me that her Daddy brought me up out of the blue and said,

"I think your mama is still mad at me. She did it again.... she brought it up again, and it's been 30 years."

A lie. A bald-faced lie. Then it dawned on me. Carter is a man who needs my forgiveness. He expected me to give it to him without asking for it. Looking back on the conversation, he said everything except,

"I apologize for it all Robin."

It's funny too, because on the day he told that bald-faced lie, I almost texted Ally to tell her Dad that I said I forgive him.

AFTERTHOUGHT

What has my life story taught me so far? It taught me to speak up sooner, to trust my gut, to keep my third eye open, to help myself, to accept help, to value peace of mind overall, that tears can be happy too, and that the child in you can weep...and heal."

I am back in therapy, and there is no shame in it. 2020- 2022 almost broke me. There were moments of complete and utter despair. I cried more in two years than I have cried all my life. I had to talk myself down more than I cared to admit. I was wounded in ways that made me lose sight of the point of living. I became afraid of my thoughts. That's how I ended up back in therapy. I hadn't talked to a therapist since the late 90s. Until this point, I was self-medicating and soothing, and none of it worked. It took the whole bottom falling out to make me finally take my healing seriously. Before that, I was just healing myself in bits and pieces here and there. I celebrated empty victories because I never got to the source of my trauma, the source of my depression, the source of my anxiety, the source of anything that I embraced that did not allow me to be fully living. I skipped over it and, for a spell, pretended that I was OK. I wasn't OK. I carried the invisible weight of unlimited tears on my shoulders. In my mind, I am always in the back of the room, watching myself knowing how detached I am. I am broken in a way that cannot be repaired. The only thing I can do is learn to live with the reality of my mother. There is no need to wonder why another does as they do. There is no need to wait and hope things work out...no need at all when you can just put the dead weight down and soar. Easier said than done. If you are reading this book, this time, I did it. I did it. I did the one thing that needed to be done, even though it is the one thing that leaves me responsible for forcing my mother to live the reality she created...where I was the prey to her glory or whatever it is that she gained for allowing me to be this way. I'm not fixed. I'm just better able to receive and process information. I am more aware of how long I dwell. I am conscious of the notion of isolation. I'm learning to foresee triggers. This is better than I have ever been before. Mine is a story of strength, perseverance, and survival that leaves me wondering why I am still here and how I am still sane. I have always had a notion of recording my thoughts, recording that spans the test of time and attests to chapters that represent stages of my life. Through literary recordings, I convey messages I set free in the air. A considerable part of my healing process involved writing my story and sharing my story freely, openly, honestly, and willingly. I was met with fear when I decided to finally lay the burden down. A fear of naming names, fear of opening wounds, fear of being the source of my mother's sorrow, fear of exposing myself to the world and showing them the side of me that makes me human and weak. The most challenging thing I have ever done was face the truth in my mother's eyes. Writing this book puts things into perspective for me. Surely it must be a lack of a mother's love that causes a woman to dismiss her child's sadness, pain, and anguish. Imagine being the child. Imagine the anguish. It's like screaming real loud, but no sound comes out, so no one can hear you. So, you block out memories too heavy for your soul to carry. Memories become few and far between.

Acceptance sets in. You accept that you did all you could do. This book was about the proverbial elephant in the room. It was about guarding the skeletons in somebody else's closet and sweeping things under the rug. It's about people accustomed to pain, suffering, and pretense on a level that creates legacies of dysfunction. It shows how like whispers passed down the line, truth becomes distorted over time and is replaced with a facade of normalcy.

The thing about "the truth" is it never changes. It can be pushed down and to the side, but it always has a way of resurfacing. People make up excuses to keep the truth a secret. The truth, for some people, is hard to look in the eyes, especially when delusional eyes must be forced open to see.

Know what you are doing when you do it. Everything that heals you will not feel good. I made a choice. All that is left are the chips falling where they may. All the preparation in the world will not prepare you to stand up to the predator that preys. If you decide to do so, be prepared. If you choose to heal yourself, and in doing so, paint people in their true light (that's not good). Be ready to be on the outside. Be prepared to have moments of utter despair from time to time. Be prepared for tears that come when they want to, that you cannot control. Be ready to be unable to look at your eyes in the mirror sometimes because some memories only make you weep. Be prepared for the fallout. The secrets you refuse to keep will tear your heart wide open. Prepare yourself for sorrow like no other because the only thing that can fix it never will. Get used to saying, "I'm

OK," when you are not. Be prepared to embrace that pain, not fight it, or just bear it. Be prepared to face the elephant in the room and know you are stronger. Be prepared to walk away from the dysfunction you call family. It is disappointing that sometimes to heal yourself, you must hurt yourself first.

The last words my mother ever said to me were, "Keep it real." How much more real can I be? The night after I confronted my mother, I cried the heaviest tears and heard the "thump" of each one. It was as though I was purging sorrow and disappointment from my being. I wept until my pillow was soaking wet. Then I woke up. Right now, I am aware that when I close my eyes to sleep tonight, it will be done. When I awake in the morn, I will know what it feels like to wake up knowing I did all I could, and now it's out of my hands.

ACTION:

I know I don't hold the monopoly on pain. Child molestations are all too common. If I know 10 women, 8 of them were molested or inappropriately touched or know someone else who was.

It is unfair that in North Carolina, a victim of child molestation must report the child predator to law enforcement no later than 10 years after they turn eighteen.

So what? The child predator is only guilty during that time frame. The law is set up to protect child predators. I mean, think about it say you were molested as a child.... then you turn 18. Most of us went to college and suppressed the ugly memories just to function. It is unrealistic to think the average 28-year-old is prepared to stand up to a predator, especially if the predator is a family member or close friend. I was 52 when I finally mustered the courage and strength to do it. I think this law is unacceptable. Something needs to be done about it

DEDICATION

Thank you to the Creator, who entered my life and was welcomed into my heart...who allows me to be...for making me, sustaining me, providing me strength, and for opening my eyes.
-Thank you to my four beautiful children, Dominique, Blaine, Marcus, and Derrick...who are all a part of me...My Loves, Motivation, Greatest Deeds, and my Life.
-Thank you to all who support, encourage, motivate, and uphold.
-Thank you to all minds open to suggestions, reflection, questions, and change, and all eyes open for sight.

Thank you to the daydreamers and dreamers who dare to dream a dream and manifest that dream into being...providing hope.
-Thank you to the ones who complete peace, embracing and providing comfortable space to share openly.
-Thank you to the Ancestors who flow freely through me, whispering in my ear when I don't know that I'm listening, reminding my soul to remember...providing the essence of me

Gratitude Always...Robin...

Deepest Thanks

A long way I've come...

A ways I have to go.

Consciously able to see me grow.

Able to look back...

without getting off track...

to see me embracing me.

Flaws accounted for...

on my list for repairs of...

Paramount things that bring light

and insight

cause I'm caring for me now.

Loving me now...

and it feels so good.

Never knew I could...

feel this way.

I opened my heart

on page after page

center stage of my life...

and you turned the pages

of my life.

If you felt me,

it's because you're feeling me

or you're going

or have gone through...

life storms...

robs the charm from your life.

 Orchestrated or implemented

or self-inflicted capers

made it possible for me to grow

and now I know that bypassing was an option

but I adopted pain after pain

in the midst of the rain in the storm...

harming me.

But I always took the time

to put it down on paper...

all the orchestrated

or implemented

or self-inflicted capers.

Because that's what I do…

write words that are true.

I felt just like I felt

I willed the words.

Some…most never heard…

except me.

And for the longest while

I wrote for only my eyes to see

and for only my heart…

I don't know when I started to share…

probably when I started to care for me.

Some folks get it.

Some folks take it wrong.

But the words belong to me…

sing their songs for me…

right or wrong they are me.

The tears flooded more than joy resounded

and I was grounded in self-pity.

One day I shook the shit outta me,

and told myself,

I could free myself of the burden

that weighed down on me…

and I found me.

I talked myself into listening and trying and

stopped all the crying

long enough to wake up…

and claim this half full cup for my own…

and vowed to never be alone to me.

Now my cup feels almost full…

and I reflect on My School of Thought

that brought light and insight…

as I try to make what's wrong right…

without forfeiting the fight.

I hear more clearly

and seeing isn't merely looking anymore…

I relish the chore of being and I'm still freeing me.

One day I told myself,

"I'm gonna write a book

that make folks look at me

and feel me

cause the electricity that flows through me

is too much for me…

So, let's share…

and at the same time care for I, myself and me…

and find clarity

and make me some cash

cause my ass stay broke…

I hope folks can feel me."

So, I got all busy and collected my papers

that held the capers that I would share.

I graduated from typewriter to computer…

but pencil and paper still suits me.

I got so juiced. I got so excited…

that I decided to take my book more seriously

and curiously it was born…

as I went through a storm.

I love to write…

it ignites me with such power

that I shower the page

with the purest of thoughts… caught in midair…

I share them with you…my gift to you…

as you see me through pain

and provide shelter rain…

cause you feel me…

and don't even know me.

As I grow,

so shall my light…

and I will always shine for you.

Deepest Thanks…

Always,

Robin Ess